Confessions of a Homegrown Alien

an Australian memoir

Jan Smith

The
Svengali Press
&

ETT Imprint

Sydney 2016

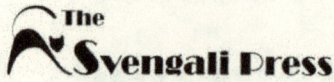

Published by

The Svengali Press
PO Box 1852
Strawberry Hills
NSW 2012
AUSTRALIA

&

ETT Imprint
PO Box R1906
Royal Exchange
NSW 1225
AUSTRALIA

ISBN 978-0-9942765-7-5

In memory of my parents

Dorothy & Randolph Smith

'This time, however, the barbarians are not waiting beyond the frontiers; they have already been governing us for quite some time.'

Alasdair MacIntyre, *After Virtue*

CONTENTS

Chapter 1
Eumundi, 1930s

Although my parents would have been young adults at the time, neither ever mentioned what they were doing around 8pm Australian Eastern Standard Time on 28 June, 1914, when Gavrilo Princip, in Sarajevo, fired the shot which was heard around the world, taking out Archduke Franz Ferdinand and his wife Sophie with a Belgian-made Browning FN Model 1910 semi-automatic, from a distance of about 1.5 metres, outside Morry Schiller's deli.

All things come to he who waits, they'd probably have said, or too many cooks spoil the broth, had either of them known the back story which led to Gavrilo standing mournfully on the sidewalk, thinking another day another disaster, at the critical moment when the royal vehicle, a Graf & Stift double phaeton, having taken a wrong turn, needed to reverse six feet in front of him.[1]

Nor did my parents know something rather more crucial, which the Archduke didn't know either. That 28 June, along with being St Vitus's Day, was the anniversary of the First Battle of Kosovo in 1389 when Serbia was defeated by the Ottomans, a most inauspicious day for flaunting Austro-Hungarian imperialism. But 28 June is also the Archduke's wedding anniversary, and only in Bosnia, an annexed territory, can his beloved not-royal-enough wife be seated at his side on official occasions.

Carpe diem, he probably said. A window of opportunity.

My mother occasionally mentioned Vienna, being fond of Strauss waltzes and tenors on our old wind-up gramophone – the records with the pink label and the mystified white fox terrier, which I did not yet know was originally called Nipper, like my own. But when Richard Tauber wasn't disagreeing that *Girls were made to love and kiss,* or Joseph Schmidt was declaring it was the happiest day in his life, *ich bin verliebt,* I knew it was bad sign, that my mother, perhaps already clutching a handkerchief, might retreat to the bedroom, and yet that it was not wholly bad, because I too could retreat to a world of imagination.

The front spare bedroom, which opened onto the porch, had a wardrobe full of clothes to dress up in, and a dressing-table with side mirrors and little drawers still bearing the scent of visiting aunts' cologne and containing my absent step-sister's discarded lipsticks and boxes of Paul du Val face powder. But the porch, which had the same white railings with slender tulip cut-outs as the more-frequented side veranda, contained an ottoman, wherein lay my father's ancient ceremonial regalia – four or five small velvet football caps in wine dark colours, edged with gold braid, from his celebrity years when he played fullback for Queensland.

Union, he'd stress, not League which was for scrubbers.

My mother had explained that ottomans were what Turkish people lay around on, and I knew a few things about Turkey, indeed the entire world, from the coloured pictures which came inside the fourpenny bars of chocolate, to be pasted in the book with the maps of the seven continents, each facing a page with ten already-captioned blank rectangles.

Ireland, the green teddy bear with the red head, wasn't entirely foreign. It was where my mother's paternal grandfather had come from, in tragic circumstances because he'd lived in the green bit which was full of Roman Catholics, which we were not – most emphatically not. Or rather, we'd ceased to be, which I did not yet understand was a different thing entirely.

My apostate great-grandfather Joseph, who'd been cut off without a penny for marrying the Protestant, was part of the foundation myth, that my mother's family was descended from Raymond le Gros, who around 1163 had been allowed to marry Strongbow's sister Basilia as a reward for successfully invading Wexford. So already I knew Papists couldn't all have been the same. In Wales, where Raymond came from, they were better, and whichever Irish he and his lads had conquered were worse than the ones who'd invited them.

My father too had been born in a foreign land, New South Wales, south of the rabbit-proof fence, where houses had fireplaces and carpets and attics, and railway lines were four foot eight inches apart instead of three foot six. So when Christmas holidays included a visit to Grandma Smith in Tenterfield, there'd be a change of trains which accentuated my father's foreignness, and the enormity of his unexplained apostasy. Conversation with my father was difficult at the best of times, and my mother knew little of football, besides it had all been when she was still at New England Girls Grammar School with his sisters, achieving her own distinction as the first new girl who'd ever asked, during the grub-eating initiation ceremony, if she could cook it first. (She was allowed to skewer it with a hatpin and toast it over a candle.)

The velvet football caps therefore trailed the same high cloudy romance and excitement as sultan's turbans, Egyptian fezzes and the yet-to-be-discovered kaffiyehs and yamulkes, as in our part of the world men wore battered broad-brimmed khaki felt hats. Maybe they had more respectable ones for weddings, funerals and christenings, but we never went to any, because everyone my parents invited for sherry and bridge was well past childbearing and thoughts of matrimony, yet well short of death, barring the usual unforseen things like being fatally kicked by horses, gored by bulls, or pinned under tractors.

And even if they were ill, I'm pretty sure none of them would have broken what for people like us was the first commandment; Thou shalt not bother Me, or Jesus who is already bothered enough. They considered us capable of sorting out problems unaided or, ideally, avoiding them in the first place though forward planning, which meant observing the next two commandments; Thou shalt build fences to contain thy flocks and herds, and Thou shalt remember to shut gates.

In Eumundi, about two miles away down the range in a wide green valley in the Sunshine Coast hinterland, where the train line ran, there were three churches, two white weatherboard, and one brown and red, all needing a coat of paint - the RCs' opposite the butter factory and the sawmill, the Methodists' up near the Post Office (shared with the Presbyterians) and St George's C of E, up the road from the blacksmith's, where we never set foot except in November, when my mother and I arranged eggs and cobs of yellow and white corn around the altar rails for harvest festival.

God also didn't seem to mind that we also drank alcohol, a word I'd never heard until I went with my town friend Joanie to the Methodist Sunday school. So I never went again, and continued to look forward to our chaste Chekhovian *soirées,* circulating winsomely with bowls of devilled Queensland nuts (not yet called macadamias) among the above-mentioned landowners, and such professionals as Eumundi could offer, namely the two bank managers and their wives. (The dentist was a Dr Connell and my mother and I saw quite enough of him anyway.)

Our previous GP had been Dr Henderson, whose son Jeremy

I'd been forced to invite to my second birthday party, but Dr Henderson had left to run a mental hospital in Toowoomba. Now it would be one or other of the two doctors who lived five miles away in Cooroy, James and Edith, who only had a baby daughter. They both told amusing stories about being asked to look at lame horses, or cows with mastitis, but I always hoped it would be Edith, who came from Western Australia and was everything you could wish for in a foreigner, slim and elegant with crimson nails, and glistening jet-black hair in a chignon, or sometimes a green velvet snood. She was also the first woman I'd seen, outside the movies, using a cigarette holder, and it was as good as watching the lion tamer when the circus came to town.[2] The minute she inserted a fresh Craven A, or maybe an Ardath, every man in the room would leap to oblige, including my father, a non-smoker.

My father and Edith, 'the quack' as he referred to her *en famille*, got on famously, especially as she'd confirmed that her home town did indeed have the pub with the longest bar in Australia, just as he'd always heard. She didn't have airs and graces like *some* people, he'd say, with the satisfied look of a husband who knows he's made himself perfectly clear.

I saw Edith professionally quite a bit, but rarely because I was ill. Our house was on top of a range, just above a perilous bend called Devil's Elbow which came after a lesser bend at our bottom gate. Even before the war, there'd be nights when I'd have fallen asleep - under the mosquito net and the watchful eye of the huntsman spider, to the sound of frogs in the lily pond, and distant curlews - only to be awakened by unaccustomed light from the veranda, and the voices of unfamiliar men. And I'd know even before I crept over to the French windows that they and my mother would be bending over some damaged person on the cane sofa, or crouching on the floor, surrounded by bowls of bloodstained water, beside someone else moaning under a blanket. Or maybe already dead.

Until the doctor arrived, there was a lot God expected us to deal with.

***

Actually we had a foreigner in our very own family who we suspected of bothering God quite a bit. We only ever saw her at Warwick in the summer holidays, agreeing with my grandmother and the other aunts, uncles and cousins that the rose garden looked better or worse than it had last summer, and it was a shame no-one played tennis any more on the old hard court by the pine trees. But even so, Aunt Madeleine, née Petracini, stood out, with her dark curly hair, pierced ears, gold crucifix and her jolly laugh.

Uncle Tom had married her a year or so before I was born, shortly after her engineer husband had blown himself up trying to fix a refrigerator in a pub, leaving her with two young sons, and because another commandment was Thou shalt never blame a man for anything (just because my mother's family had stopped being Catholics didn't mean they'd stopped being Irish), at first it was seen as ensnarement. But over the years revision set in, at least she wasn't an *Irish* Catholic, maybe it had been one of the better hotels, not a fish and chip shop, that her parents had owned, and after my cousin Billy was born, the rare times fault was mentioned it was the bank's, for sending a mere boy of twenty-four, their youngest-ever manager, to somewhere as godforsaken as Georgetown.

Billy told me the Petracinis had come from the Dolomites, which sounded much wilder than the Italy of the chocolate atlas, with its Ponte Vecchios and Trevi fountains.

'Poor Mum, they expected her to have a stiletto tucked in her garter.'

Nobody minded that Billy was prone to exaggeration, that

6

too was expected of Italians, along with being musical, and when it was time to gather around the piano in the big room with the wicker chairs and the Georgian silver tea and coffee pots on the sideboard, he never failed to oblige. But every so often, instead of some harmless Edwardian ditty, *Lily of Laguna, Daisy, Daisy,* or *The Daring Young Man on the Flying Trapeze*, Billy would carry us into unknown and passionate territory with *La Donna E Mobile*, doomed gypsies, tragic and unseemly Puccini, and rousing Handel, before taking us safely back with *Danny Boy,* and *Oft in the Stilly Night*, to fond memories of the way things used to be, or should have been, in Ireland. Or before the later *naqbas*, the war which was supposed to end all wars, and the Depression.

My unmarried uncles also played a cultural role, showing us kids their big art books with the lissom naked boys, and naked women, especially those in perilous situations – Andromeda chained a rock, whom they assured us would soon be freed by Perseus, and the blonde being unchained from a tree by a knight, which before too long I'll know is similar to the stained glass window Philip Marlowe observes in General Sternwood's Los Angeles mansion, thinking the knight is taking rather a long time about it.[3] Sometimes there were goitrous women wearing floaty garments and glazed expressions, to whom my uncles paid little attention. But there was also a gaunt terrified man about to eat a tiny adult, which they told us was a Greek god called Saturn who'd devoured his children, about which I undoubtedly made some sensible observation, like wouldn't it have been easier to eat them when they'd been babies, when they'd have been tastier? Why had Goya made them so shrunken and passive?

But the uncles didn't linger over that either, or the primal cause of this aberrant behaviour. As one doesn't, when it involves castrating your father.

***

The best thing about summer holidays in Warwick was that I could venture even further into Italy, metaphorically speaking. Aunt Madeleine always went to Sunday Mass with her three boys, so nobody dared say I couldn't go too, apart from a few feeble warnings that it would all be in Latin. Paradoxically that was a help, I could give more attention to the bells and smells, the painted plaster Virgins and the bleeding hearts, which in this new context looked altogether more magisterial and numinous than did the tiny replicas I'd occasionally glimpsed in other people's houses above their moquette sofas and rows of china shepherdesses, while standing hesitantly on their doorstep, or awkwardly in their kitchens accepting a store-bought biscuit that wasn't a gingernut - the only exception to a further commandment, A woman shalt bake her own biscuits, and never buy gravy or custard powder.

Little did we know that by 1943 we'd be seeing Italians back home, all year round, pairs of maroon-clad men amidst the alien sugar cane and pineapples when we drove down to Nambour. But everyone agreed they were poor harmless souls, the Germans had dragged them into it, and more fool them when everyone knew Italians couldn't fight their way out of a paper bag.

There was no mention of stilettos, or unseemly passions.

***

The chocolate atlas wasn't the only impetus to exploration. There were also the novels my mother kept in the glass-fronted bookcase, the Georgette Heyers and Daphne du Mauriers, Elizabeth Goudge's *Green Dolphin Country* (exotic New Zealand) and others involving romantic attractions on tea and rubber plantations.

The bookcase itself was another thing which wasn't as my mother would have wished. Nearly all our furniture had come from Trittons - the dining table with the lollipop legs and the six chairs, the sideboard and the three-piece lounge suite, and her writing desk against which the 410 gun and the 22 rifle leant, handy to the bullets and cartridges in the drawer alongside the good bridge cards. All of it no doubt the cat's pyjamas in 1929,and bought by perfectly respectable people, but for people like us, even my father's family in Tenterfield, there was another commandment, Thou shalt inherit thy furniture.

The fire had happened on a Monday morning, 11 November, 1929, a date already associated with endings, when a neighbour had burnt off lantana on a windy day, sparks flying up the gully and lodging in our ceiling while my mother and the laundry girl toiled over the washtubs under the house. So my father was summoned too late, and with the water pressure being too weak, everything was lost, the piano and nearly all her wedding presents, and for the next six months they'd lived in the barn.

Some days I'd pretend I was living there too, in a snug corner among the corncobs and the rusting ploughs, smelling the mice. Had there been a carpet snake in the rafters? What had they cooked on the little pot-bellied stove? She never said, but always looked displeased. Yet the barn-dwelling period was what Donald Rumsfeld would one day call a known unknown, for even at age three I knew that it was here, enclosed by the cobwebby walls, that my mother drew the first rough sketches of the wonderful new house, and the resplendent garden, knowing it would be powerless to erase the spirit of the woman who haunted her in the old one.

Of course there were unknown unknowns, not all of them traumatic. Indeed, sixty years on, I'll be blown away to find that in Arabic the words for gestation, gardens, enclosed spaces and invisible demons all derive from the same three root letters, JAN.

**

Beyond the barn there were paddocks with creeks, guava

bushes, and tawny orchids spilling from dead tree trunks, to be explored whenever I wanted, on foot or astride Paddy, my step-sister Sheila's pony. But Paddy was a truculent geriatric, sometimes rising to a brief trot if she ran behind him with a switch of camphor laurel, and no way could he be taken onto the main road, which sadly involved another commandment, Thou shalt not covet thy neighbours' buggies and sulkies, nor cadge rides therein.

The best I could hope for was a trip to Nambour in our green Hillman sedan, my father coasting down the hills to save petrol, past the gumtree with the warning, *Flee from the Wrath to Come! Jesus Saves* while I imagined myself galloping on a foam-flecked pony down some thrilling side road. And one memorable day we actually did turn off, onto a dirt track flanked by pineapple fields, to visit the Swiss family Staub. Mr Staub was one of the exotic people my father had met in the Top Pub, and while my mother and I admired their wooden cuckoo clock, we secretly thought Mrs Staub could have made her coloured rugs in half the time if she'd held her knitting needles properly. And when afternoon tea appeared, we could scarcely contain our amazement.

Twelve eggs to make a cake!

But the most mysterious place of all was Kenilworth, where every month my father went alone, in a blue shirt with long sleeves requiring cufflinks and elasticised silver bands. I now know this was for meetings of the Kenilworth Farmers' Co-operative, and there is primary evidence (my mother's diary, a school exercise book with a shiny dark blue cover) that I was sometime quite distressed, like a cat when a suitcase is taken down from a shelf.

Kenilworth was about twenty or thirty miles west of Eumundi, up the Mary Valley, and one thing I knew, you'd know when you got there because there was a there there. Kenilworth was an actual town, whereas Doonan, Verrierdale, Belli and Eerwah Vale, despite the signposts, didn't really exist. Not that it stopped me imagining that once upon a time there'd been a Patrick Doonan or a Monsieur Verrier, a Jacques or a Francois like the romantic Frenchmen in my mother's novels.

After all, my mother often took me out into the garden to look at the stars, where nobody had been either, and the Big Dipper was definitely there, like a saucepan with a handle. Its proper name was Orion's Belt, she said, after some hero in a Greek myth who'd been fatally bitten by a scorpion which was also up there somewhere, though harder to see than the Pleiades, the seven weeping sisters which even the Aborigines knew about.

Little did my mother know that a real Monsieur Verrier, (Urbain Le), predicted where an Englishman would discover Neptune on 23 September, 1846 although today they're claiming that Galileo saw it in 1612 or 1613, but with a very small telescope. But it was the Frenchman who suggested the name Neptune, or better still, Le Verrier, forgetting that pride goeth before a fall, and like Napoleon, (right there on our biscuit tin, triumphantly astride his rearing white horse) Le Verrier lost out. The world chose Neptune, the god of the sea, and even in China and Japan it's called something which translates as 'sea king star'.

***

At some stage before Nick Koufalakis started his Blue and White Café, next to the Bottom Pub, there must have been another foreigner in town, because of the jar of curry spices which had long lain undisturbed in our kitchen cupboard. My mother agreed the little seeds and bits of bark smelt wonderful, but she'd gone on buying Keen's curry powder because there was no way to grind them up. Lord knows they'd tried, my father putting some in the vice we used for cracking Queensland nuts, only to wind up with smarting eyes, and cranky as a bear with a sore head for the rest of the day. Which her diary notes he quite often was.

Nonetheless, I'd soon invented the storyline, an Indian hawker needing help with a broken buggy shaft or axle, or an incomprehensible notice from Maroochy Shire council; my father, as the local JP, summoned from the pub and given the spices by way of thanks, and me an instant passage to India.

It even became a story-within-a-story, whenever I'd read my kids the Janosch story about a tiger and a bear who found an empty banana crate with 'Panama' stencilled on it. 'Panama smells of bananas!' the animals cried ecstatically, resolving to set sail as soon as possible.

But one foreigner remained a mystery, whoever was responsible for the fragment of a nursery rhyme, already garbled by transmission, learnt from my mother, *ria ria runka, hessel vara rubbleshack* while she bounced me on her knee. I'd have attributed it to some long-ago nursemaid, but in Warwick all our maids, in the days when we'd still had them, had been lumpen Irish girls who had to be taught how to lay a grate, clean silver, hang shirts on a line and fold sheets properly. (Another commandment, Thou shalt not ask thy servant to do anything thou knowest not how to do thyself.)

Perhaps one of them had spoken Gaelic?

***

[1] David James Smith, *One Morning in Sarajevo: 28 June 1914,* Weidenfeld & Nicolson, London, 2008.

[2] Dr Edith Hill died aged ninety-seven, in Brisbane, on 2 April, 2012.

[3] 'I stood there and thought that if I lived in the house, I would sooner or later have to climb up there and help him. He didn't seem to be really trying.' Raymond Chandler, *The Big Sleep,* Alfred A Knopf, NY, 1939.

Chapter 2
Origins

At 9 o'clock we were abreast of the point distant from it 1 Mile, depth of water 14 fathom. I found this point to lay directly under the Tropick of Capricorn and for that reason call'd it by that Name. Longde 209 O' West. -Captain Cook's Diary, Friday, 25 May, 1770.

***

Captain Cook, no stranger to climate change, therefore knows that within a month he'll need every woolly undergarment sensibly packed by Mrs Cook back in Yorkshire where the sun, probably obscured by milky grey clouds, will reach its northerly limit, 0 degrees Cancer, marking the official mid-summer.

That's what the Enlightenment's all about, he tells himself. Understanding things which appear paradoxical, or rarely but predictably. Praise God last year in Tahiti visibility was excellent for the transit of Venus, as the next one isn't until 1874.

But in Eumundi (Latitude 26S23, Longitude 152E48), and on most of the planet, people knew one thing that wasn't remotely paradoxical, but bleeding obvious. That when men went off doing heroic things for king and country, or science or God – humanity and democracy being way in the future – it was their wives who kept bread on the table, ran the farm or the business in between ensuring the kids kept their noses clean and rugged up well, said their prayers and minded their ps and qs.

So if anyone had said otherwise we'd have thought them a shingle short, and reminded them of yet another proverb, it's a wise child that knows its own father, never dreaming that one day we'll be told it can be solved overnight by a DNA test.

On a mundane, physical level, my father was very much visible, and even down in Eumundi there were fathers who came home every few hours to keep up their strength and converse with their families at the kitchen table. But due to my father's deafness his contributions were unpredictable, largely depending on what was in that day's *Courier-Mail*. This arrived every day around half past three, flung into the dusty red-iron-roofed cream box by the paper man who drove up from Brisbane, and who'd later deliver me as well, after a humiliating phase when my father had driven me down and collected me, waiting patiently in the green Hillman sedan. Afternoon tea – raisin-studded rock cakes, apple teacake and Anzac biscuits – thus became a continuation by other means of my formal education at Eumundi State School.

This, my first victory over authority, had begun two years ahead of schedule, as I was reading by age three, aloud on my father's knee from the old pink *Bulletin* or curled up with one of my mother's rare indulgences, *The American Women's Home Companion.* A large glossy monthly, this was far grander than the *Australian Women's Mirror,* already (still?) socially inclusive with readers' recipes and homely anecdotes about people muddling through, and a children's page where I sometimes won a certificate for writing little paragraphs, whereas the *Home Companions* were aspirational, and strongly focused on progress and efficiency.

If *Modern Times* ever screened at the Eumundi School of Arts we wouldn't have gone, as my mother wasn't keen on Charlie Chaplin. But I've yet to meet anyone who didn't know the now-iconic image of him in overalls, crunched between two factory wheels, is a metaphor, and you're supposed to feel sorry for him. Yet there, in one of the *Home Companions,* was a story without a hint of compassion, running over several pages, about the timetable a well-organised hostess should follow to ensure a successful dinner party – at least a dozen little clocks alongside drawings of her checking the casserole, arranging the flowers, and lying down with slices of cucumber over her eyes, though I imagine at some stage she'd have checked the rest of the magazine, to see what to say about serious social issues.

Abortion is an Ugly Word.

In contrast, the *Courier-Mail* offered scant hope of the world becoming a better place. But on the rare days when some government, federal, state or local, hadn't done something to set my father off, useless bludgers making country people's lives a misery, there was usually the consolation of *schadenfreude*, or rather plain old unconfined *freude*. Men he'd gone to school with at Kings, or better still men known to my mother, who'd died leaving barely enough to bury themselves, just as he'd always known they would, or having their fingers burnt doing something any fool could have told them would end in disaster, usually involving livestock, land or investments.

There were also reports of unknown men charged with interfering with children, exposing themselves or 'using an instrument', but these were more the province of *Smith's Weekly,* which luckily for me was more interested in straightforward crimes like murder, men chopping up their *de facto* wives or being dismembered themselves and fed to sharks, usually in Sydney or Melbourne, which ensured many happy hours in one or other of my cubby houses. I had one under each tank stand, and by the shadier one my mother had created a little rockery, so because another commandment was, Thou shalt tackle the hardest job first, on Saturday mornings there'd be real blood, dripping down on the violets and maidenhair fern from the beheaded chook which would become Sunday lunch.

My father too had a bookcase, just outside his office in the breakfast room with the yellow-pebbled windows overlooking the back garden, so as well as puzzling over the instrument users and the interferers, I puzzled over gestation, gelding and oestrus. There were also books about pigs, because he'd once tried breeding Berkshire whites, but the only survivors from this star-crossed phase were two large white sows in a pen by the barn, and the pigwhacker beside his rolltop desk, an instrument with a bamboo handle and two square leather flaps at the end, which I never saw him use on a pig or any other creature, though adults, and of course Ian and Sheila, found it amusing to say he'd use it on me, if sufficiently provoked.

The Smiths were what they now call 'notables', as evidenced in the collage above the desk, showing a property outside Tenterfield called Aldershot, an enormous place with lawns and trees encircled by a stone fence, a veritable New England Tara. (The School of Arts had been packed for *Gone with the Wind*, my first grown-up movie). But what I mostly looked at was the main photograph, of Lady Linden, one of Grandpa Smith's racehorses, winning the Newmarket at Flemington in 1932 (27 February, at 33 to 1). Hollywood and social constructs had nothing to do with it, because it wasn't until 1944 that Elizabeth Taylor rode The Pie to victory in *National Velvet*. In my case it was obviously hereditary, even manifest destiny.

Even the wisest child is lucky to know about any of its great-great-grandfathers, and unless they're egregiously good or bad, or it's convenient to pretend they were, or still are, fathers and paternal grandparents rank a distant second in the narrative we hear from our mothers. So it wasn't until the 1980s that I heard about Robert, the ostler of Tunbridge Wells, who had a way with horses and women. In 1826 he allegedly eloped with Henrietta Driver, his boss's daughter at the sawmill, but this cannot have been too serious, as they remained in Tunbridge Wells for another twelve years and had three children before coming to Australia where Robert got an offer he couldn't refuse from the Hon. Edward Ogilvie. Leaving Henrietta in Sydney to get on with having her baby, Robert and the two older boys, George and Harry, now ten and seven, relocated several thousand Ogilvie cattle from the Hunter Valley to the Clarence River, where Henrietta had her seventh and last child in between pulling beers, selling flour, sugar and tea and being postmistress at Fairfield on the Drake goldfields.

My informant even gave me a photograph of Henrietta, taken after the death of Robert who'd soon acquired his own spread at Cheviot Hills, and shortly before she'd married George Minto Brown, aged twenty-seven, the children's tutor. Henrietta was then around fifty, as was I, so it was pretty inspirational, even if I wasn't into younger men.

With all one's teeth, or most of them, who knew what might be possible?

***

Not once did I ever see my father on a horse, not even Sandfly, the bay filly he bought for my tenth birthday from Roy Duke out Kenilworth way, though admittedly she wouldn't let anyone near her but little girls - she'd previously been abused and the necessary whispering had been done by Roy's daughter Glennie. But I knew genes could skip a generation, and if I never got around to wondering why my father had all those horse-breeding books, that's what happens when a girl's in love - name me one great fictional detective who ever was. I loved Sandy passionately, even after she bolted and threw me over a wire fence - six inches higher and I'd have been a goner. But my mother accepted full responsibility, having just handed up a bunch of flowers in crinkly white paper - which naturally was delivered to my teacher within the hour, because that was another commandment. Anything short of breaking your back, if you didn't immediately get back on you'd be called a sook forever.

Glennie the horse-whisperer was also brilliant at maths, as was my father, and regularly topped the year while I only came second, despite nights of misery being told what to do with sines and cosines, based on what he'd been taught to do with them by teachers who weren't deaf, forty years earlier. But on Saturday afternoons he was like every other father, coming in from mowing the lawn to listen to the races, (me already glued to the radio, studying the form guide). Otherwise, in memory anyway, he was usually under a car, or bent over a piece of machinery in a smallish space smelling of axle grease and petrol where tools – pliers, soldering irons, vast families of spanners – have to be put back in their proper place.

But my father was the only son, and going on the land was Smith males' manifest destiny, as it would have been in his mother's family, the Stewarts, too, genes or no genes, if the only Stewart son hadn't died at age twelve (at boarding school, of diphtheria), leaving my grandmother Alexandra Stewart and her five younger sisters to carry on the tradition, leaping sidesaddle over five-barred gates and distinguishing themselves at the Tenterfield Show.

My mother too had cleared a few fences in her day, and claimed she'd been the first girl on the Darling Downs to ride astride, in a smart riding coat and jodphurs. Whether her mother-in-law Alexandra was scandalised, or furiously jealous, or possibly both, I never discovered, but there were certainly *issues,* because in my mother's eyes it was Grandma Smith who was entirely responsible for condemning my father to a cow town like Eumundi.

'Grandpa Smith was quite a nice old thing.'

I was eight when he died, but that was already my impression too of Harry Avery Smith, mild-mannered and harmless in a suit which had become too big for him (unlike my Warwick grandfather, he'd shrunk with age), sitting on a sunny bench by the honeysuckle creeper, puffing a pipe. He probably *was*, there wouldn't have been room for a patriarch and a matriarch in the same house, and by 1954 it's clear from Alexandra's obituary in *The Tenterfield Star* that she ran everything else, the Countrywomen's Association, the Red Cross, and even the Border Caledonian Society – the first woman in Australia to head any Scottish Society.

But *her* father I'd been hearing about for as long as I could remember, the curmudgeonly Sandy Stewart of Millera who was anything but a nice old thing, and whom my mother, who also knows about heredity, holds responsible for everything that's wrong with me.

Sandy (a named he loathed) was born in Dollar, Scotland, and also wound up on the Drake goldfields, as a hawker. The part-time gun running and sly grog making was a later discovery, along with his wife Mary Anne being the daughter of Charlie the deer-poacher of Essex and Isobel the watch-stealer of Inverness. There was a foundation myth with the Stewarts too, that Sandy sent all six daughters back to Scotland with ruby necklaces, to induce chagrin. Untrue, and pointless too, as his other ten siblings (eleven counting the eldest half-brother packed off to Canada at his mother's breast, that we didn't know about until 2012) had all done equally well. But entirely typical, as Sandy definitely had the gene for *schaden*-free *freude,* though it could well be a characteristic a man acquires through having six daughters

The happy years he spent, forever needing to challenge some young pup to race him down rocky mountains in thunderstorms, or to ford flooded creeks. And why not, when he'd had all six girls taught to play the piano, hauled in by a bullock team through leech-infested forests, and instructed in painting by Tom Roberts whom he'd persuaded, around 1895, to stay for several months?

***

The most interesting period in anyone's life is the decade before we were born, and for the normal run of people, it's not wars and what they fought each other for, but the personal stuff, how and why we came to be born at all - what our mother and father (assuming they actually *are* our biological parents) were up to, and whether we were conceived in hope, desperation or negligence. And in my childhood all I knew regarding my father was that after being a celebrity footballer, he'd been packed off to clear a family property at Tumblegum, from where he'd run away to Roma and either driven a taxi or mucked about with cars, probably both, until he was despatched around 1915 to Eumundi, the new big thing where Harry Avery Smith had just bought four hundred acres of prime dairying land.

But beyond this it was like whatever lay at the end of the roads down which we never travelled, a dark hole in my personal landscape made even darker by silent witnesses. Because out in the far paddocks, beyond the one where we kept a few milking cows and Paddy the geriatric pony, were two dapple grey Arab mares which nobody ever rode, Sister Olive and Sweet Lady who'd belonged to Kathleen, my father's first wife, whom nobody ever mentioned, except to tell me she'd died of pneumonia.

Not surprisingly, the *Women's Home Companion* considered only children a very serious social issue, but even if Kathleen had made my plight a little less serious, how could I possibly be *spoilt*?

Too many toys? Why did I need any when I'd long ago graduated from my doll and the two stuffed rabbits to Nippy the fox terrier, a succession of poddy calves, tortoises, and tomcats reconstructed by my father's teeth after the application of rubber bands? Only children also got too much pocket money, which they spent in drugstores on ice-cream sodas, whereas all I got was fourpence on Saturday mornings for an ice cream at Nick's Blue and White Café, and whatever the educational chocolate bars cost at Brandon's grocery.

Things were clearly very different in America. Different too from the England of the Milly Molly Mandy books (my usual Christmas present, with a hanky and a cake of soap), where only children explored copses, spinneys and water meadows, and any new dresses were run up at home, as mine were, by their mothers on a treadle sewing machine.

But what definitely ruled out spoiltness were Ian and Sheila. Whenever they came home from Gatton Agricultural College and Brisbane General Hospital, they couldn't wait to pull my plaits and call me Jamtin, swearing my head rattled like an empty one with stones in it, or teach me to ride a bike, with a gleeful shove so they could watch me crash into the nasturtium bed. To this day I can't stand capers. For a while they'd aimed me at the outhouse, covered by thick soft honeysuckle, but my father feared for its stability so it was back to not being a sook in the nasturtium bed, and identifying with fictional heroines, or actual princesses like Good Queen Bess, who'd survived a wicked stepsister.

My father too sought solace in novels, a stack of them on his side of the double bed, but to me they were of little help. Unlike my mother's, his were set in Australia in the here and now, or fairly recent past, and written by atheists or Irish Catholics who lived Down South with trade unionists, voted Labour or even Communist, and did things nobody we knew would have dreamt of doing, like roaming the countryside, picking fruit or peas and worrying about poor people. It was all very puzzling, especially when my father got a bit choked up, the way he did at parties when he wanted people to sing *At the Balalaika* after he'd had one too many. Or when my mother was away in Brisbane having some operation.

'There's some women who understand how a bloke feels.'

Obviously he saw something in these alien women which was more important than their politics and religion. And whatever it was, my mother didn't have it, which didn't necessarily mean that Kathleen had had it either, though I knew she'd have been as good a catch as any of the Stewart girls and probably better than my mother, being the daughter of the rich and famous Barneses of Canning Downs.

The only difference I could see was that my mother, on marriage, had put away her jodphurs and riding coat, and Kathleen hadn't. Otherwise Sweet Lady and Sister Olive wouldn't have been out there in the far paddock, silky and silent reminders like the late Rebecca de Winter's underwear in the drawers at Mandalay.

At the time I thought the second Mrs de Winter was a bit of a sook, too, not realising that life will soon imitate art.

***

By now Pluto, the latest and furthest planet from Earth, had become a source of innocent merriment, in Walt Disney cartoons, but while the dog's adventures changed every week, with planets it was history repeating itself.

In 1915 the Lowell Observatory photographed two very faint images of some as yet unrecognised object (as had several other people, possibly as early as 1909), which on March 13, 1930, was scientifically proven, by acting director Clyde Tombaugh, using a blink comparator, to be a planet.

Percival Lowell's widow Constance favoured Zeus, or failing

that Percival or Constance, but the observatory, long at loggerheads with Constance, took a democratic approach. More than a thousand people wrote in and again it was a win for foreigners – Venetia Burney, of Oxford, England.

Why not Pluto? says Venetia to her grandfather. The god of the underworld who was able to become invisible, and whose realm equates so well with the dark cold reaches of outer space? As one does, if one's grandfather has been head librarian at the Bodleian and has a brother who's already named the two moons of Mars Phobos and Deimos. *Persephone*The closest I'd got to Pluto was being shown Dante Gabriel Rossetti's, and asking if it's so hot down there in Hades, how can they grow pomegranates?

None of my family had ever laid eyes on a pomegranate, but the uncles probably chuckled and said you'd better ask Aunt Madeleine, she'd be the expert. That's the trouble when you're an eleven-year-old girl, even back then adults never gave you the full story, those warm human details about castration and cannibalism and being abducted by handsome dark strangers in black chariots, thinking you'll be distressed, when nine out of ten eleven-year-old girls would love to be taken away from their mothers, whether or not they've reached the stage of having anyone specific in mind. Heavens, if I were eleven years old now, when it's a proven fact that girls mature earlier, I'd have been thinking half her luck if Pluto looked like Johnny Depp.

Meanwhile, in Arizona, it's possible Tombaugh didn't know the details either, but he knew one big thing, that the first two letters of the name Pluto would make the perfect glyph because they'd stand for Percival Lowell – otherwise Venetia would never have had her fifteen minutes of fame before she too became invisible until around 2009, when the media ask what she thinks about Pluto's demotion.

At her age she doesn't much care, she says – hardly

surprising, unless by 2003 England expects even nonagenarian English gentlewomen to burst into tears or sue somebody. But I bet she was a tad moved back in whenever it was that an asteroid was named the 6235 Burney, and a spacecraft instrument, hitherto called the Student Dust Counter, was renamed Venetia.

***

Chapter 3
WW2: Working for the Yankee Dollar

During the *Risorgimento*, the reunification of Italy which since the fall of the Roman empire has been provinces behaving according their needs and natures, Garibaldi, or possibly Cavour, visits Sicily to expound on the glories of Italia, the future nation state

'Who's Italia?' one peasant whispers.

'Must be his wife,' says the other one.

***

As well as the nights when my mother tended bloodied and broken bodies, there were also entirely predictable ones which were different from all others, when we'd curtsey three times for luck to the new moon, looking over our shoulders and making a secret wish. But on 4 September, 1939, it was still a week away, and though for once we actually were gathered around the radio after dinner, like the families in the *Women's Home Companion,* there the similarity ended, my mother bursting into tears and my father shouting 'What?' even before Neville Chamberlain said no such undertaking had been received.

Wishing was not going to help.

As Hitler rampaged across Poland, we cut a map of Europe from the newspaper and pasted it above the radio, to be stuck with pins. As your heart is pierced too, years later when you see other people doing the same and have to wait until you're outside - Heather Kennedy and myself, the hardened journalists, blubbing in the sun by the Prinzengracht around 1970. But the things you couldn't see, only sense, went on just the same only more so – women whispering and then falling silent, smiling too brightly when they saw you.

One day when everyone had gone out to one of our other farms on Mineshaft Road to pick beans, then bringing an unheard-of fourpence a pound, I found my mother sobbing in a way which was different too.

'The *Hood* went down', she said, looking away and pretending to do something with her famous mince pies.[4]

Our green Hillman was a hardtop sedan, she'd hardly have been crying about anyone else's, parked there alongside it in the shade where she was setting out the lunch. So someone must have recently arrived, perhaps some pregnant neighbour not up to strenuous labour, with sandwiches she'd made while listening to the radio.

Pretty soon Saturday mornings became work too, standing beside my father outside the Bottom Pub, collecting old kettles and saucepans to be taken down South and turned into munitions – bullets, bombs, perhaps even Wirraways.[5] It was what communities did, all hands on deck, shoulder to the wheel and pitch in, but back then we weren't aware we were one, simply that we'd become Australians united against one common enemy, and then against two after the Japanese bombed Pearl Harbour in December 1941.

But by February 1942 they were bombing Darwin, so sometime between then and July, when they bombed Townsville, we went back to being Queenslanders again. Those perfidious Southerners! And sure enough in a few decades they'd be telling us the Brisbane Line never existed, it was just our *perception*. As if Queenslanders didn't know geography when we saw it.

Soon it was only little kids like me going to school in the mornings, the older ones went in the afternoons, all of us having fun in the two zigzag trenches my father had organised a team of men to dig under the camphor laurels, longer versions of the one he'd dug at home under the ficus hedge bordering the orchard.

My mother had been busy too, preparing for a different bombshell, where sadly I was not present, which suggests it was in the morning that the man from the ministry called, regarding the aircraft observer my mother believed was about to be billeted with us. 'I expect your man will be quite comfortable in here,' she said, (or says she said) showing him the front spare room. Perhaps flinging open the wardrobe, now emptied of my dressing-up finery, and indicating the washbasin and tap in the corner, while the man from the ministry wondered if they'd made some terrible mistake in the selection process for the Volunteer Air Observers Corps.[6]

The breakfast-room windows and the top of the back door, with the panes of white, orange and yellow pebble glass, were already been covered with blackout paper. But within days the door had two big flip charts as well, our planes and theirs, Zeros, Mitsubishis, Kawasakis, even Messerschmitts and Stukas, handy to a stack of thick block pads with sections for noting height, speed, direction, wind strength and cloud formation, estimated wingspan, number of engines, and markings if any.

At first my mother was forever rushing into the garden, wet- or floury-handed, even in her petticoat, leaving me to take over whatever she'd been in the middle of – plucking the chook or making the butter while keeping an eye on the cumquat marmalade. Sometimes it was the worst possible moment for me too, just when I'd been hoping to hear more about the men in the photographs she'd been showing me, the wonderful tennis players who'd danced divinely. But I was soon entrusted to handle the entire event, short of the actual reportage, being not yet tall enough to reach the telephone. And though I secretly longed for a Zero, the most exciting it got was the twin fuselage

Lockheed P38, which my mother reported without feeling the slightest need to insist (as we heard other observers did) that she hadn't touched a drop all day.

***

Uranus, the previous most-distant planet until Neptune, was also discovered by an Englishman, German-born William Herschel who was organist and choirmaster in the Octagon Chapel, Bath, when he wasn't holed up in his shed. He spent about sixteen hours a day there, a proto-Steve Jobs, while his sister Caroline, scarred in infancy by smallpox and stunted by typhus (she was four foot three) acted as housekeeper. Or so it was long believed. But it's my bet that on that night in March 1781, Caroline wasn't indoors making jam or knitting comforters, she was right there beside her brother, in the back garden of his house in New King Street.

At first they thought it was a star or a comet, but clearly it was beyond the orbit of Saturn, the serial child-devourer in my uncles' art books, which patrolled the border between the visible universe and the divine. And happily Herschel showed some respect, wanting to name it George in honour of the King. But it was soon declared a planet, and named Uranus after Saturn's father, the sky god who invented a million marvellous things every day and when ninety percent proved not to be marvellous, as usually happens, buried the mistakes in the body of his long-suffering wife.

The French, the traditional enemy of England and now of monarchs as well, kept calling it Herschel for a while, but the George was a brilliant idea, as within a year George the Third appointed Herschel King's Astronomer, and Caroline too found a new career as a professional singer, mostly Handel soprano roles. She also became the first honorary female member of the Royal Society, after discovering several stellar bodies, and had an asteroid and a moon crater named after her.

***

Until the troop trains began coming north, the Eumundi railway station had been a stop on the way to another killing field in the opposite direction, wherever it was they sent the poor poddy calves. They were already the colour of blood, glossy little Herefords with a white face or blaze, the more determined ones protesting and pushing their wet noses, the colour of erasers, through the slats, and the weaker being trampled to death inside.

The railway station was down behind the CWA rooms, where on Thursday afternoons my mother presided at the Comforts Fund, while my two town friends and I helped out with afternoon tea and sampled other mothers' cakes and biscuits. These no longer had pink icing because cochineal, along with cuffs on men's trousers, had been banned under the austerity regulations, but we'd always offer to wash up, knowing that when the knitters resumed their navy and khaki scarves and socks, they'd discuss even more alarming changes.

In Albert Street, from Saturday mornings until the small hours, they'd heard there were queues stretching three blocks or more. Not the Negroes, of course, they had their own place across the river, and you could just imagine what sort of women ... but men had to have their fun, poor devils, black or white. Trust the wowsers and the parsons to make a fuss. But on some Thursdays far worse things were happening not a hundred yards away.

Thanks to Miss Norma Edwards of Nambour, where we went by train on Saturday mornings, Joanie and I were proficient tap-dancers. We could also sing quite pleasingly – *Mairzy Dotes, We'll Meet Again*, and whichever version of *Give Me One Dozen Roses* the situation required, usually the Australian one, whose next line was 'put the Yanks in a steamer, and send them back to

29

USA'. So as more and more troop trains came through, the pennies mounted up, and on days when it was Americans, our takings increased exponentially.

But money wasn't the issue. We'd made ourselves cheap, particularly me, who should have known better, and though it was never spelt out, the really cheapening thing was to have done it in front of foreigners, not Nick Koufalakis in the Blue and White Café, or the Staubs down at Palmwoods who couldn't help being different, but Americans, people who'd had every opportunity to learn how to do things properly, given they too had started out as an English colony, and wilfully chosen otherwise. It was more than the understandable confusion of florins with pennies, it was part of an overall failure to remember that more is less.

It's not until the 1970s that I hear this is attributed to Mies van der Rohe, though I suspect it's yet another thing which gets discovered every few centuries, and that we weren't the first people, either, to realise that for a gift one is always beholden, if not resentful as well.

***

Our own private Americans were also people my father had met in the Top Pub. Maybe they'd heard about the four ravishing barmaids, the Misses Ball, and figured it was worth the drive up from further down the line where they were doing something unmentionable in a forest. Not selling all your eggs to the Egg Board was something best not mentioned either, it was strictly illegal.

'Fifty dozen a week they reckon they'd get through,' my father persisted, as my mother grappled with her conscience. Even I could figure out that if there were fifteen men, it amounted to a dizzily excessive six eggs per man per day. So the next Saturday there they were, roaring up the paddock in their jeep, startling the cows and stopping at our garden gate under the scarlet bougainvillea trellis. And there were we, trying to forget *Rum and Coca-Cola*. If anything set my mother's teeth on edge, it was the Andrews Sisters.

Both mother and daughter, Working for the Yankee dollar.

The one in charge – American rankings were still puzzling, and they always called him 'Chief' – was a Southerner, so my mother, already shamed at having fallen into trade, was at war with him even before the kettle boiled, and not because he wasn't like Rhett Butler or Ashley Wilkes in *Gone With the Wind*. It was only on Saturday nights we ever saw aborigines, the Whittakers and the Wilsons, who always sat in the front left side row on the hard chairs with their smaller children and the dogs curled up underneath, but in my mother's eyes the colour of the driver left sitting outside in the jeep was immaterial. He was a man, or rather *men* in the collective, military sense, and for people like us there was another commandment, Thou shalt attend to thy men and animals first.

The Chief kept saying there's no need, ma'am. My mother kept ignoring him, and despatched me with tea and homemade biscuits on the same china she was using for the rest of them. Like Chandler's knight liberating the naked lady, I too took rather a long time about it, standing there marvelling at his perfect teeth and the immaculately pressed and tailored uniform, but worrying too, about the black lines on his palms. What if the horrible Chief made his life even more miserable for having dirty hands?

On these fraught Saturdays, my next obligation would be the conducted tour, setting off with one or two of them, not much more than boys, from places like Nebraska or Iowa, to show them my pet bantams, Dick and Daisy, in the yard with the big privet tree, then the cow bails and the barn, ideally with a resident possum so the carpet snake would be in the stables, with luck draped over the bags of shellgrit and chicken feed so I could be impressively heroic and poke him with a branding iron until he slithered up into the rafters. I forget whether this got me an actual Hershey Bar, but I'd recently been given *My Friend Flicka*, and the best reward was enlightenment about pintos and palominos, and how a Spanish saddle differed from ours.

Meanwhile my mother would be showing the others around the garden, her pride and joy – the lily pond made by my father from half a corrugated iron tank, ringed with portulacas and sweet alyssum, lawns extending past squat date palms, poppy beds bordered with ranunculus, a sweet pea trellis, and several permanent trellises of dense tropical creepers, rangoon which we called quisqualis, pink coral vine, speckly Dutchman's Pipe and orange bignonia venusta. But if they'd already returned to the front veranda steps and the ornamental chillies – red, purple and orange, and ferociously hot – we'd find her going another round with Chief.

We understood perfectly that boys would be boys, but Chief would say it out loud, winking about a little fun in the mess tonight, showing he couldn't control his men, let alone himself, probably not even when sober. On Saturday afternoons he never was, so my mother's final battle would be with my father, for offering him one for the road.

***

By 31 May, 1942, the Japanese had snuck three submarines as far as Sydney, so who could say they wouldn't swarm ashore at Noosa Heads any minute and it'd be far worse than a few plates and pictures crashing to the floor. The fuss Sydneysiders made, simply proving they were soft buggers, malingering with aches and pains they'd never have known about if they hadn't listened to commercial radio. So we slept more soundly once there was an

32

army camp just up Sunrise Road, with a clear view of Noosa across the mangrove swamps.

Our *soirées* now happened more frequently and became even more Chekhovian, with dashing officers lighting Edith's cigarettes, my mother's too, and bringing us mud crabs writhing in hessian sacks stuffed with wet leaves. There were also precursive glimpses of Tennessee Williams' gentlemen callers, maybe the wonderful tennis players and divine dancers themselves, or men who'd known them, and once a month, a sewing bee in our breakfast room where staid farm wives would giggle and roguishly slap the knees of total strangers from Fitzroy or Carlton. I hadn't heard a woman laugh so much since Aunt Evelyn came up to have Dr Connell take all her teeth out.

There was a family curse with teeth as Aunt Evelyn can't have been more than thirty, though most Australian women had them out around forty, and some even before marriage to save their husbands the expense of dentures, which I'd like to see as another instance of Irish misogyny. She lay in the second-best spare room for weeks where I'd read her Lennie Lower stories until she'd beg me to stop because laughing made her gums hurt. The only one I remember, probably because it involved deep ethical questions, was where Lennie and his mate, adrift in a lifeboat with a woman, give her all the water so they'll be too weak to row.

In civilian life the sewing bee men had all been tailors or in the rag trade, so their jokes may well have been the ones I'd be laughing at myself before too long. The fortune teller who is undismayed when the girl she's predicted will marry a brain surgeon runs off with a butcher, and the *shadchen* who points out that the prospective bride only limps when she walks. Perhaps they even told what would be my husband's favourite, about the shop with the watch hanging outside where they don't fix watches, but castrate cats.

At camp concerts the jokes were visual as well, men in red wigs with balloons or footballs stuffed down the front of their dresses doing obscene things with broomsticks, my mother sitting beside me on the rug in the dark, giving the odd flinch and occasionally whispering 'boys will be boys', as if she might be still smiling after the laughing had stopped. But it was sad, too, knowing she was thinking of the soldier in the photograph, in the turned-up slouch hat with the feather, and his silver cigarette case and her letters they'd sent back after Passchendaele, and how the officers and the tailors, now cavorting merrily, might soon be dead too.

New Guinea was another thing my mother knew about, like cochineal being made from beetles, and the taste of white grubs, because she'd gone there after WW1 with her father, an old friend of some district commissioner. I'd sit there stroking the white-spotted wooden pig with the tail that stuck out straight, while she told me about women with a baby on one breast and a piglet on the other, thinking that was sad too, it didn't make up for her parents not letting her go nursing in Flanders. It wasn't her death they were worried about, it was the fate-worse-than. They believed that women who nursed soldiers were next door to prostitutes, or she'd end up like Garp's mother and rape a dying man.[7]

As I've said, you don't stop being Irish overnight, and my mother would be telling me soon enough there's no such thing as a bad man, only bad women who lead them on.

***

At our *soirées* and sewing bees, men were in little danger as any younger married women were quite often pregnant, including Doctor Edith and Sheila who'd come to live with us while her husband was off fighting in North Africa. If any single women disappeared for a few months, I'd never have noticed – at age seven, it's an exciting business watching someone turn you into an aunt. It's now believed that Nurse Luke, who ran Eumundi's Sunny Brae Hospital, kept a little black book, but by the 1940s it hardly mattered. As people said, you'd have something to remember him by.

Edith sometimes came on holidays with us at Caloundra, where we'd relocated the Noosa beach house. It was usually rented out and we'd stay opposite, across Tooway Lake in what would now be called a trailer park, though domestically the cabins were a giant step upwards, with mains electricity supporting a toaster, a jug, and a microwave-sized cooker. But at home we had a kerosene refrigerator, and here it was just an icebox, replenished every few days by a cheery leather-aproned man we called Likeahoven, because he'd always tell us how hot it was outside. There were also bakers who delivered, and a milkman about whom I could see nothing ribald, not yet knowing that in England, where my comic books came from, milk was delivered much later, when husbands were at work.

***

The end of the war was certainly Plutonian. My cousin Ian Fairbairn hadn't died after all on the Burma Railway, he just hadn't been listed when the camp was liberated, because he and some mates had already escaped and had been hiding in the jungle for a few months. We all went to Brisbane, my mother and Ian's (Aunt Trudie), dear old Mina, various cousins and me, but I was considered far too young to meet the ship as they expected him to be all skin and bones like the people in Belsen.

Ian was soon back home on Malvie Downs, up in Julia Creek, so I only got to know him sixty years later, at Mooloolaba. Before we went to the cinema he told me he actually hadn't looked too bad, after several weeks in a Bangkok hospital and then the sea voyage. Teeth held up amazingly well, too, he said, confidently disimpaling kebabs at the Turkish restaurant, which was how the subject had arisen.

After the movie I could see I'd got things wrong too, persuading him to see the George Clooney film, which wasn't all that good, because he'd dozed off quite a bit and when it was over he said he'd have quite liked to see the one with Toni Colette and the Japanese tourist. But never again did he mention the Burma Railway, or Changi either, and at his funeral in 2011, attended by several politicians and climaxing with a flyover of the Wirraways he'd once flown, it appears that nobody else had ever got to hear a word either.

***

[4] HMS *Hood*, a battlecruiser and pride of the Royal Navy, was sunk by the German battleship Bismarck on 24 May 1941 between Greenland and Iceland.

[5] The manufacture of aircraft required virgin aluminium.

[6] By May 1942 the VOAC, initially attached to the Directorate of Intelligence, was controlled by the Directorate of Pursuit, Fighter Sector HQ, Allied Command.

[7] John Irving, *The World According to Garp*, Corgi Books, London,1978 and filmed in 1982 starring Robin Williams and Glenn Close.

Chapter 4
St Margaret's 1948-1951

Sheila had been packed off to St Margaret's well before age twelve, which I now was, and for years I'd been dressing up in her old navy uniforms with the distinctive middy blouse and white collar. If I'd gone to Nambour High School I might have married a boy like Kevin Rudd and it would have been history repeating itself, cut off without a penny like my Irish great-grandfather.

The very first day status anxiety threatened, the portly widow in charge of the West dorm in the old Hall telling us we were no better than common vulgar factory gels. But when you've helped win WW2 your self-esteem is in fine fettle, just as well as she told us every second day regarding untidy drawers, wrinkled brown lisle stockings, or imperfectly mitred bed corners, and I was even a little smug, as people like us never uttered either word. It would all be conveyed with an imperceptibly raised eyebrow or a tiny shrug, and if we'd ever met a factory girl, a whole different set of rules would have applied, she might have been a rough diamond, or one of nature's gentlewomen, another term I never heard, though there must have been if there were natural gentle*men.*

Besides, with 'common' and 'vulgar' I suspected there was some subtle yet crucial difference, as with those *faux amis* we were warned about in French, *magasins* which weren't magazines but shops (though nothing was said about places where Arabic-speakers store guns and provisions).

Then, three months later, I became a displaced person. My father was building a new house at Caloundra alongside the old one, my mother wrote with *faux* enthusiasm, attempting to beguile me by enclosing rough sketches. It wasn't bad, but still, my green paradise was gone forever, my pony too, never again would we discover six exciting things before breakfast – mushrooms, dead crows or wild blackberries in the bushy lanes – or race home before a thunderstorm broke, never caring if it did. The smell of damp and grateful grass mingled with wet leather and sweaty horse, equal to yet different from that of the curry spices and the banana-scented crate from Panama. A decade later, when they tell me about adrenalin, I'll feel smug about that, too.

***

The only glimpse of paradise at St Margaret's was the cardboard boxes of *petit fours* which the more affluent parents arranged for McWhirters, the nearest department store, to deliver every Saturday. Even today, resolutely passing *patisseries* on my pre-breakfast walks, all it would take to stop me would be a tray of little green-iced frogs with tiny chocolate eyes.

Naturally there was a resistance movement, where someone would climb over the plywood partition into the storeroom and steal enough bacon, eggs and butter for a fry-up in the laundry, which had a gas-jet for making starch. I just hadn't realised, until the Class of '51's first glorious reunion, forty years on, that it was usually me, so it's probably true, as it's well known that incarcerated people have total recall of their gastronomic miseries – fried liver tough as an old boot (Thursday breakfast) and powdered scrambled eggs (Tuesday and Friday).

We were only sprung once, after we'd had to put out a fire and some kid went and blabbed about her burnt gym tunic. But it only resulted in a weekend detention, of little consequence as boarders were detained already, and some feeble attempts to shame us – St Margaret's didn't do guilt. (The first time I read the word 'guilty' outside a courtroom context I'd gone back to the beginning, thinking I must have missed something.)

Another identity change was discovering we weren't Protestants, but Catholics. *English* Catholics, so you could say things changed yet remained the same. The school motto, embroidered on our blazer pockets, was *per volar su nata,* but that was to remind St Margaret's girls that they too were born to fly upwards, and the rest of Dante's sentence, lamenting mortal man's tendency to be overthrown by little winds, was never mentioned.[8] Still, it's hard when you're the only girl in the class without an embroidered blazer pocket.

We only encountered Dante in English and History, so his concept of the afterlife topography remained unexplored. What did St Margaret's girls need to know about a purgatory which didn't exist, and a paradise full of saints who had no business being there? In a few years there'll be many people eager to enlighten me, but all they ever remember is the *Inferno*, who'd ended up there and why. Which in the case of Guido Bonatti and others of his kind they said was perfectly obvious.

Thou shalt not suffer a witch to live.

Not until the next century do I hear about the nine circles, where Dante discovers Guido Bonatti in the eighth, (in the fourth ditch, or *malebolge*, thereof), one level up from Jews and Muhammad, and that his sin was actually fraud, pretending to be a Franciscan monk.

***

St Margaret's didn't burden us overmuch regarding sin; the worst thing was being seen in the Pig and Whistle, a milk bar in Queen Street frequented by the faster daygirls. To me they all looked perfectly capable of dealing with boys, especially Denny Lawton who conducted us in *HMS Pinafore*. The only males we boarders ever saw, apart from a bronzed tennis coach, were ageing gardeners and whichever dentist or doctor justified being on the fully-escorted tram trip to the city on Monday afternoons. But by the time I'd cracked my front tooth, and needed glasses to see the blackboard, let alone Mr Right, there were higher priorities than boys.

My major discovery, apart from the shop assistant in Woolworths who said it was all rubbish about tampons destroying your virginity, was a health food shop in Adelaide Street. Back then yoghurt came in only one flavour, plain with undertones of goat, but I'd pretend to enjoy it, idling by the bookshelves where there was abundant confirmation of the far greater perils of just about everything on the St Margaret's menu. Anything from a packet or bottle, white bread, margarine, jam, tapioca and sago (as in the pudding we called frog spawn) and best of all, the detestable saveloys and frankfurters at weekends.

With tea and coffee there was also moral peril, they stimulated 'animal passions'. Not just the chicory essence kind in the Camp bottle which would later become a collectible – the Gordon Highlander hovered over by his faithful turbaned servant in darkest wherever it was – but even the real sort my mother made, steeped in a small red enamelled jug and served half and half with warm milk.

Alcohol, tampons, coffee. Why were they always telling you things that weren't true?

One thing we boarders knew about animal passion, or the initial steps, it didn't necessarily involve boys. The two teachers who canoodled every lunch hour under the jacarandas on the front lawn didn't look entirely ridiculous, in fact quite *luxe et volupte*, but it was still depressing. An Australian *boy* who'd read poetry? Or who'd lie with his head on your lap, gazing dreamily upwards, and let you read poetry to him? We'd sit there enthralled, eyes and then heads slowly swivelling ever further from whatever revolting substance was on our plates, until we were brought to heel by whichever teacher presided over our table. Though there was fun to be had with the younger and prettier ones.

'How's your boyfriend, Miss? Does he read you Paul Verlaine? Baudelaire?'

My second cousin Deirdre, the kindergarten teacher who'd just become engaged to an up-and-coming architect, fared rather badly.

***

The girls who took Art, along with my Warwick uncles and possibly even General Sternwood over in Los Angeles, would have known Aquarius was once associated with yet another lissom lad, Ganymede the cupbearer to the gods. But in 1789, the discovery of the first extra-Saturnian planet was as big a paradigm shift as the twin fuselage Lockheed Lightning, and while some argued that it made no difference, if God had thought we needed to see any more planets with the naked eye he'd have made them bigger, the prevailing view was that it stood to reason that by permitting us to see Uranus with a telescope, God was trying to tell us something. That once again humankind had been weighed in the balance, and far from being found wanting, as was usually the case, had been judged ready to move on.

And so began the exciting new task of re-shaping a planet in our own image, and what can you do with a castrated god but think positively and focus on his core strengths? Clearly Uranus was the green light for inventions, revolutionary changes, industrially, politically, even theologically (was God really necessary?) and Ganymede must be reconstructed as something closer to Prometheus, delivering not fire stolen from the gods, but the waters of knowledge to which humankind was now fully entitled. Never mind that in my uncles' art books Zeus has had

Prometheus chained forever to a rock to have his liver pecked out by eagles every night, because it grows back again by next morning. (How negative can you get?)

Of course it's arguable that all this new scientific knowledge attributed to Uranus, notably Benjamin Franklin demonstrating that electricity results from the connection of positive and negative forces, was simply what people were more disposed to notice, the way you never realise there's so many pregnant women, or people in plaster casts, until you're pregnant or injured yourself – though how do you get in either condition if not through sex and sudden dramatic events? Would there have been quite so much of both, with a planet called George?

One thing's certain, by turning Uranus's weakness into his greatest strength, Benjamin Franklin paved the way for the Age of Aquarius.

***

The most mortifying thing was that the Sisters of the Sacred Advent didn't look like real nuns, the ones down the road at St Rita's, or from All Hallows. They didn't look like Ingrid Bergman either, but they wore big black belts and crisp white headgear, whereas ours dressed strictly for comfort in rumpled navy cotton habits, and wimples which had never felt the bracing kiss of starch. It was rumoured they weren't even required to shave off their hair, or not completely, so in chapel there was no point in gazing at the novice and imagining some lover left to sorrow over her shorn locks.

There was only ever one, very plain, so I imagine none of us were too surprised that after 1962 there were hardly any girls wanting to be real nuns either. But back then we'd have been regarded as amazingly prescient if we'd said we could have told them so or, a decade or two later, whenever it was they started saying 'one door closes, another one opens', that often it's the same old door being opened by different people.

Walking through Kings Cross one spring day, in the late 1990s, I ran into the much-married ABC personality Paul Macleay, about whom I've long known more than he suspects, from the afternoons in the 1960s when I'd enjoy animal passions with his flatmate, and then raid his bookshelves and pleasure each other yet again, reading aloud his copy of Elizabeth David's *Mediterranean Cooking*.

Paul looked pretty stricken, as I supposed any man would if his daughter had gone off to become a Buddhist nun.

'Well, daughters tend to do these things,' I say. Me, the mother of sons, open to persuasion that things could be worse.

'But she's my *wife*.'

Until then I'd always thought the worst mortification for a man would be a wife just plain walking out, with no man whatsoever in mind, but by now, I could see that a wife in love with an invisible man must be infinitely more humiliating.

***

On Sundays, in St John's Cathedral, we'd line our shoes with damp blotting paper in the hope that we'd faint and be carried over to the Deanery to be revived with sherry by some handsome young deacon. Even the girls doing physiology did it, who must have known full well it wouldn't drain blood from your head. And by 1958 I'd discovered the Deanery did indeed have a handsome Victorian sideboard, abundantly stocked, and the newly-arrived Dean William Baddeley would have been ideal if he hadn't already been married to one of our distant English cousins.[9]

It was this side of the family which had produced the three Royal Apothecaries, but by 1860 my great-grandfather Thomas had refused to be the fourth. Contemptuous of the bourgeoisie flocking to his father's door, he'd come to Australia where he'd fathered three children, a son and one daughter marrying a daughter and a son on the Irish side. So those of us who were double cousins soon knew there can be competing narratives regarding that term once beloved of historians, *wie es eigentlich gewesen,* how things actually had been. The delicious stories dear old Mina would tell me, how her father/my Great Uncle Jack had arrived in Warwick, circa 1890, to seek the hand of her mother, and been met on the platform by her brother, Uncle Wilfred/my grandfather, wearing spats in the middle of February!

Regarding ecclesiastical refreshment, two of us finally got lucky. Knowing a statue of Our Lady of Fatima was in Brisbane, one Monday afternoon we'd got as far as Holy Trinity in Fortitude Valley only to be told, by a nice man in a windcheater with a turned-up collar, that we were a week too late. And we'd thought he was just a gardener seeking shelter from the rain.

'Two little Protestants!' he kept saying, as we struggled to recall which pope had exclaimed *non anglii, sed angelii* on seeing the little blonde slave boys.[10] Yet another of Our Lady of Fatima's miracles, to be celebrated in his office where he'd lend us a spare umbrella.

The rain kept pelting down, we were there for ages drinking whisky and talking about the man both sides of my mother's family believed had been my grandfather's cousin, who'd once led the Irish Home Rule Party. Even about our invasion of Wexford in 1168, not something I'd normally have mentioned, but an excuse for the present invasion seemed a good idea. And as nothing much was said when we staggered back to St Margaret's, it suggests I invented another credible excuse, about dentists or sluggish trams, or that Our Lady of Fatima watches over Protestants too.

But *mea culpa,* Father, about your umbrella.

***

Only two or three girls did German, maybe because they too

had mothers who'd go all weepy and reproachful, 'after all our poor boys have just been through'. But in the late 1940s it was what everyone had just been through that was at the bottom of most things.

Everybody knew a war widow, or some poor soul whose husband had returned limbless or deranged, who had to work to avoid being dependent on some pitiful pension. Indeed dear old Mina, who'd been forced to sell the farm and become a school housekeeper, was still waiting for a pension from the war before. If husbands came home syphilitic and shell-shocked and eventually hanged themselves in the barn, it was the fault of those Mademoiselles from Armentieres, nothing to do with the Australian government.

But well before *The Prime of Miss Jean Brodie,* in 1961, St Margaret's girls could also see that the men who hadn't come home, the invisible ones, were responsible for a few things too. It wasn't just Dante and his 'born to fly upwards'. Far from being thrust upon us, as they now believe, shorthand and typing (let alone 'home economics' – what Australians knew as domestic science) were only for the C stream girls, not the Bs and certainly not us *crème de la crème* A girls. If anyone's to blame for my invasion of the commercial block to peck away on the C class's Remingtons, it's Hitler.

Shortly after the war a Eumundi neighbour had been visited by her sister who now lived in Canada. She'd got out of Germany around 1936 but still kept in touch with the family where she'd been a *Haustochter,* (a sort of duty-free *au pair*) so next thing I'd acquired a penfriend, Annemarie von Something, who wrote me perfectly typed letters in near perfect English, and it became a question of honour.

I was soon caught out by Mrs Kelly, the commercial teacher, who within minutes was showing me how to place an envelope slantwise across the keyboard and telling me stirring tales of former pupils, particularly one Lorraine Stumm, who'd become war correspondents, which would never have been possible if they hadn't mastered shorthand as well. This, plus the music lessons, meant my hands were never idle, and it was in the music block that I discovered Denny Lawton wasn't as bad as I'd thought, and had a mother just as awful as mine.

***

At Caloundra, nothing will convince me it didn't rain every holiday, miserably in the winter and in late summer malevolently and cyclonically. I'd moved on from Gregory Peck to mooning about Robert Mitchum, whom my mother couldn't stand, read endless Agatha Christies and suffered tragically with Tchaikovsky, though on a clear day I might sulkily tag along to watch her enthuse over sundry flotsam – a huge but tragically dented tin of ham, and with luck another big green glass ball from a fishing net, to be artistically arranged beside the others, and giant claws which had once scuttled across the seabed.

Solitary expeditions were much more fun, exploring the rock pools in the hope of discovering a yellow-brown suckered tentacle of an octopus which with a few sharp prods might emerge and create some excitement. In late winter, the breeding season, they were especially ferocious.

The old couple next door let me use their dinghy, so I'd check other people's crab pots in Tooway Lake and often row right to the end, past dense banskia and ti-tree, imagining myself covertly observed by an Aborigine or some amiable hermit. Our only winter visitors were another ancient couple, tweedy English people with a brace of smelly spaniels, who played bridge and talked about India. It wasn't until summer that there were landed families with sons home from boarding school, (along with my childhood *bête noir*, Jeremy Henderson), any one of whom could well have been Mr Bingley, had I not been the wrong Miss Bennet.

One blessing was that when Great Aunt Effie Bernays died she'd left me her pianola, the one I'd loved to play at Cleveland in the crepuscular drawing room opening onto the creeper-covered verandahs, imagining Effie and Charlie playing duets before walking hand in hand down the freesia-scented terraces to the soggy lawn where the white picket gate opened onto the oyster beds.

Uncle Charlie, a marine engineer, had died before I was born, but in a family whose womenfolk were unaccustomed to romance he'd assumed legendary proportions, a veritable Mr Darcy, the flower of civilised English manhood who'd proposed to Effie within days of falling in love with her at a grand ball at Government House, and who'd dropped her off at church to play the organ and then walked to the end of the point and back in time to escort her home. Who'd been to Russia to oversee some marine infrastructure and been given marvellous presents by the Czar.

Who had inherited these, if they'd ever existed, remains a mystery, and I didn't get the actual pianola, either, which was traded in for a small new Belling upright. But just as Chandra Lal's spices had once transported me instantly to India, all it took was one minor scale to put me in to some candlelit drawing room in nineteenth century Europe, with an eighteen inch waist and unencumbered by the hideous glasses, conversing fluently in three languages, like George Sand/Aurore Dudevant/Merle Oberon in *A Song to Remember,* with talented men in crumpled white neckcloths, who'd possess all the virtues of Uncle Charlie and could suffer from any disease they liked, even consumption, as long as it wasn't deafness.

***

47

In my final summer holidays I was sent to Sydney where my widowed Aunt Trudie, my mother's elder sister in Bellevue Hill, had extensive connections. Our living-room walls at Eumundi, and now Caloundra, were hung with excellent watercolours she'd done before she'd got married, so after thirty years on a sheep station in Julia Creek it wasn't surprising she'd reverted to culture, which in 1950s Australia effectively meant converting to other people's.

In my father's opinion, any woman who'd begun life as Gertie should have stayed that way, not turned into *Trudie,* a reffo name if ever there was. Little did he know that Aunt Trudie also served reffo vegetables, chunks of corn on the cob and broccoli with white sauce, in a pair of elegant silver dishes (Aunt Effie had not forgotten her, either) and *gugelhopf* from something called a *patisserie.*

To acquaint me with my well-heeled paternal kin, Aunt Trudie had taken me to visit the last of the six Stewart daughters who'd married the survivors of the trials by ordeal. My father didn't hear half of that either, and my mother nothing at all.

Whether it was Beatrice or Maud who was bedridden in Manar in Macleay Street I'm not sure, but there was a bunch of fearsomely sophisticated grandchildren - some no longer landed, but stockbrokers or lawyers, or about to be, and already engaged - and eventually she was propped up with pillows to sort through the years and fill us all in on who'd done what to whom.

Most of it was known knowns, my father's flighty cousin Eve Mocatta, the far more spectacular divorce of Aunt Linda from Uncle Reg in the 1920s, and how, after Grandpa Smith's money had all but gone on legal fees, she and Uncle Reg married each other again and found Jesus.

But suddenly it was 'Randolph, that shocking business with poor Kitty, oh those poor little children, finding her like that'.

I stood there in my newly-made pink linen dress, trying to look as if I already knew about that too. The former lover who'd wanted her to run away with him, otherwise he'd tell my father about what she'd had, or maybe hadn't had, years ago in Sydney, and Ian and Sheila, aged nine and seven, being sent to gather eggs and returning too soon, and 'Poor Randy coming back when it was far too late', when she was arching horribly on the kitchen floor from the strychnine, and telling him she didn't want to die after all.

***

[8] *O gente umana, per volar su` nata, perche' a poco vento cosi` cadi?* Purgatorio XII.94-13. 'Oh mortal man, born to fly upwards, why does such a little wind o'erthrow you?'

[9] The two actresses, Angela and Hermione Baddeley, later revealed he was only their half-brother, probably the son of one their mother's actor lodgers.

[10] 'Not Angles, but angels,' attributed to Gregory the Great in 573.

Chapter 5
University of Queensland 1952-3

The bourgeoisie has subjected the country to the rule of the towns. It has ... rescued a considerable part of the population from the idiocy of rural life. -Karl Marx, Communist Manifesto.

***

The worst time at Caloundra was the shameful trudge around the neighbourhood trying to cadge a lift back to Brisbane. I forget what the train fare cost but the process started at the bus station, where it was usually my father who bought the ticket and Mrs Watson, the wife of the proprietor, would look considerably friendlier than when it was bought by my mother.

'Maisie McTiernan that was', he'd told me, with the nearest he ever got to a conspiratorial wink. 'Used be a barmaid in Roma'. I hadn't realised women who knew how a bloke felt would turn into stout matrons wearing crucifixes. So the day I found myself sitting next to Mrs Watson on the bus to Landsborough, which meant sitting beside her on the train to Brisbane, it was my father's past I was hoping to discover, not the need for radical change in my immediate future.

'Never!' said Mrs Watson, aghast. 'A daughter of Randy Smith's, working in a *bank*?'

I said I didn't fancy it either. She'd already told me about the jolly nights in Roma - did I know how well he could sing? Not a car in the district, either, that he couldn't fix, what an engineer he'd have made! But in the excitement of sitting next to a woman I'm convinced was once my father's mistress, (hoping for another glimpse of rosary beads when she opens her handbag to offer me another store-bought biscuit that isn't a gingernut), it takes a while to notice the subtext. References to parental failure to recognise their children's talents, the achievements of her daughter Marie the Commerce graduate.

I explained that I'd dropped Latin after two years and hadn't done science.

But surely I was doing Economics?

Only a couple of daygirls did Economics, with Miss Horton who also taught Ancient History, in an unforgettable dress with horizontal rows of tiny flamingos. No way would she let me start halfway through September.

But yet again Mrs Watson reached into her capacious black handbag, perhaps with a quick silent prayer as her hand slid past the rosary beads, to produce one of Marie's old textbooks she'd been intending to give to St Vincent de Paul. So it became another question of honour, a flung-down glove like Annemarie's typed letters, leaving no option but to get up at three for the next two months to hole up somewhere with a torch and a stash of stolen bread, figuring out why something went up when something else went down.

***

I don't know whether my mother knew who was responsible, or that I was probably the youngest person who'd ever got a Commonwealth Scholarship, but she cried quite a lot that Christmas, and not just because Commerce equated with being in trade, whereas working in a bank didn't – even the art-loving uncles had done time, to understand pastoral management. It was more university *per se,* which people like us had absolutely no need of.

I knew Nancy Mitford's father, Lord Redesdale, had thought so too, and that too much education made girls dowdy, but many Australians had qualms too about harmful influences, look at those men reduced to hawking clothes props in the Depression, half of them Arts graduates! As well as being sullied by trade, I'd end up unsuited to be the wife of anyone except some Commo who wouldn't hold with marriage anyway.

But conspiracy theories, no. It wasn't until I was actually there that I heard the four year Latin prerequisite for Arts students (which survived in Queensland long after other states had dropped it) was just another Papist plot, to disadvantage Protestants.

In 1952 the University of Queensland was still relocating to St Lucia, where an imposing sandstone edifice concealed workmen's sheds, concrete mixers and huge piles of sand. Only the engineering students, the despised 'greasers', were still back in George Street.

There didn't seem to be a soul from St Margaret's. Either they'd taken up teachers' training scholarships, undeterred by the prospect of years of indentured labour in some place like Julia Creek, or Georgetown, or they'd had enough science to do physiotherapy and be on the Herston campus with the medical students. Admittedly there were two other options for the under-Latined and unscientific, but Surveying was boys only, as field trips would have posed insuperable difficulties, and my glasses ruled out Physical Education.

Under the Colombo Plan, Asians could study at Australian universities provided they went back and modernised wherever they'd come from, and around a third of Economics 1 was dainty, almond-eyed, glossy-haired girls with names like Nakanopakoon. But Professor Gifford was rumoured never to fail a blonde, and though most of the Anglo Six were blondish already, we always sat at the front, never failing to laugh at his jokes and imagining that his jolly wink, whenever he said 'Gentlemen!' was just for us.

Anyway, we all got a credit or better.

***

For obvious reasons no Misses Nakanopakoon did Arts. Apart from a few boys in corduroy trousers who read poetry, a couple of priests and a disagreeable man in a wheelchair, it was full of blondish girls in pleated flannel skirts, cashmere twinsets and the *de rigeur* brown and white Saddlemaster shoes. Every morning a small group congregated on the steps, smoking black Sobranies and expounding on Karl Marx, Kant's categorical imperative, and Superman. They didn't look the sort who'd read comics.

But hadn't I just spent four years doing Shakespeare, poets from Chaucer to Wilfred Owen, both Brownings, all three Brontes and Jane Austen? There'd be the rest of your life to read once you got married, even to write books yourself. What did city women *do* all day? (Thanks to WW2, my concept of good works had never developed beyond knitting.)

The big thing back then was 'educate a woman and you educate a family', obviously doomed as the Arts girls all swore they couldn't even boil an egg, and found babies disgusting. They didn't even seem interested in sex, whereas I'd sensed possibilities after a dirty old man had run his hand up my leg, trying to tuck up my dress so I could help him hunt for yabbies in the creek. I hadn't obliged, but the distress of my mother, who believed him to be a pillar of the community, was not unenjoyable. I'd even read van de Velde's *Ideal Marriage* by torchlight under the bedclothes with my cousin Dora in Warwick.[11] What problems could there be?

Psychology 1 therefore seemed a good idea. I'd soon worked out that Superman meant Nietzsche, but who was this person called Freud?

***

In Psychology 1, God was definitely dead, and whatever else might have created a world in which everything, one way or

53

another, had babies every spring was conspicuously absent. The new divinity was science, now expanded beyond physics and biology, the discovery of radium and heliocentric universes, to include *social* science, which every day, in every way, was enabling people to *progress.* Upwards and onwards, freed by higher education from the ignorance of their superstitious ancestors.

Proverbs were particularly scorned, as one often contradicted the other and in the brave new world of social science there was no room for ambiguity, much less paradox. Either a thing was or it wasn't. In two years we never got past rats, statistics and tortured baby monkeys, and there wasn't a word about Freud. Except that Mrs Freud had been a Martha Bernays. With Uncle Charlie, I'd always assumed distant French ancestry, thinking of Bearnaise sauce.

'Why didn't you tell me? I asked my mother. Secretly chuffed and sensing a major *schadenfreude* opportunity.

'What does it matter?' she said, after a slight hesitation. 'He was always a perfect gentleman.'

I resorted to telling Cousin Billy, hoping he wouldn't mind his mother being eclipsed. How was it possible that our family never suspected the reason for those solitary walks to the jetty and back, while Aunt Effie sat at the church organ playing *Onward Christian Soldiers?*

Not that I thought Uncle Charlie's origins should have been immediately visible. Thanks to Economics 1, I soon enjoyed a special relationship with Zell Rabin in Economics 11, who'd begun life in Vilnius and knew no Latin whatsoever. He was blondish with quizzical blue Paul Newman eyes, enough for every girl, perhaps even the Misses Nakanopakoon, to be secretly in love with him if he hadn't also been doing Physical Education, going around in shorts and expertly dribbling a ball down the parquetry corridors while giving us sly smouldering winks. The boys in the corduroy trousers never made us feel like that. But paradoxically it was perfect, knowing Zell was forever beyond us because he'd been betrothed since childhood to a girl called Lillian Roxon, in Sydney.

Nonetheless, whenever Zell sat down beside me and drew diagrams in the sand to illustrate yet another something which went down when something else went up, (more or less frequently, or more or less suddenly than something else) I strove to be worthy of his attention. What if he switched to mentoring one of the other Anglo Six? Never must he discover I'd never laid eyes on a five pound note until I was at boarding school – some daygirl's father being conspicuously charitable – and had only lately realised all those whsl mfrs in the telephone directory weren't because postmen were forever losing their whistles while fleeing savage dogs.

Zell also edited *Semper Floreat*, which soon ran a page one story referring to me as Miss Independent Front Suspension. I hadn't known what that meant either, as my father never explained cars any more than he did football, and if anyone had told me Zell was responsible I would have disbelieved it, or more likely forgiven him. As I would also have forgiven David Malouf, whom I've only recently been told was co-editor.

***

One of the many things in Psychology 1 which had been scientifically proven was that there were only five senses. For whatever it was that enabled my pony and other creatures to foretell earthquakes, there was merely anecdotal evidence, a very bad thing and even worse if it came from people who believed in water divining.

Like everyone else around Eumundi, when a new well was needed we'd call in a man who'd walk around holding a bent wire until it started twitching. But in Psychology 1 rural people meant Jukes and Kallikaks, snaggle-toothed families in the Ozarks with too many cross-eyed kids, sitting on the porches of shacks with dead rabbits nailed to the posts. The sort I'll soon discover they'd only just stopped wanting to sterilise.[12]

In Political Science and Economic History they knew about rural people too, though here the focus was on wicked capitalist landowners. But any images were invariably of the urban sort, Georg Grosz's sausage-necked Germans with shiny bald heads and pudgy features, not the pre-war kind with the fur coats and hooked noses. So progress wasn't always bad.

***

Just after Orientation Week, I'd sighted a Psychology 1 girl at the other end of the virtually empty toast-rack train carriage. She was from Somerville House, but being glad to see even a remotely familiar face, I hitched up my skirt and strode across the intervening seats to sit next to her.

'*You'll* get on,' she said, drawing own skirt closer.

Somerville House, for Methodists and Presbyterians, had even more daughters of the *nouveaux riches* and aspirant *bourgeoisie* than did St Margaret's. But Ruth wasn't one of them, as pretty soon she's telling me she'd been accosted by some frightful person with a clipboard, conducting something called a questionnaire, and wanting to know the occupation of her grandfathers. 'But they didn't work, she'd said, only to see the frightful person twice tick 'unemployed'. (Later she'll tell me one had been an honorary consul in Peru, which sounded a pretty gentlemanly pursuit, not too onerous).

Obviously people like us were in serious trouble, so we soon became friends, united against a common enemy.

***

The ice-maidens of the sandstone steps also spoke

authoritatively on the class struggle, and in the temporary structure grandly known as The Refectory, over a lamington or a stale Eccles cake, I'd keep my ears open on how to assume a new identity. There were two options, both useless.

A few confessed that sometimes, being short of money, they'd spent part of the summer vacation in Northgate Cannery, wrist-deep in pineapple chunks alongside girls as rough as bags. By second year, after scouring saucepans and cleaning lavatories in a hotel at Mooloolaba, I'd discovered the teasing could be punctuated by random acts of kindness, but even so, why would girls born to indoor flush toilets and beach houses at Surfers want to apostate? If the Mooloolaba girls were any indication, the working class wouldn't be fooled for a minute.

'You swallowed the dictionary? What's Economics when it's at home?'

What if they found out about the racehorses and the posh schools, the Georgian silver teapots and the three Royal Apothecaries who'd prolonged the lives of profligate and oppressive monarchs? I'd be swinging from a lamp-post in two shakes of a lamb's tail. And that wasn't the worst of it.

Even back when we'd been Papists, as dear old Mina still called them, it seemed we'd been the wrong kind, the man on the right side of Irish history had been Michael Collins. Exactly how we'd set back the cause of Irish freedom for decades I never discovered, because Arts-Law, the only faculty with men who weren't Asian, or returned servicemen in drip-dry shirts, (a sure sign of a working wife), or disabled or wearing corduroy trousers or into Jesus, was an Irish Catholic heartland.

It's true Arts-Law boys would start out telling me about The Troubles, but when whoever it was eventually woke up, in the small hours in his father's car along Toowong Reach, it would be time to go home, none the wiser and with my virtue intact. So although you were always hearing that priests told them they were free to try their luck with Protestant girls, Catholic boys were actually safer.

Paradox was alive and well, despite Psychology 1.

***

By second year, my economic problems acquainted me further with the middle class, which as I suspected came in more varieties than were officially acknowledged. Sometimes I'd be ironing white shirts for unseen husbands whose occupation was a mystery except that they were 'in business'. But all of them wore underpants, an item of clothing I'd never dreamt existed. Neither did I admit, when I wasn't out ironing, that I'd never listened to the Argonauts, couldn't sing the Aeroplane Jelly song, and hated Vegemite. Nor would wild horses ever get me to say *toilet*.

I still saw Mrs Watson occasionally, in her office near the exceedingly genteel Shingle Inn with the waitresses in Olde English floral uniforms. Her occupation was unclear, too (I think it involved trade unions), but much was said about the advantages of joining the Australian-American Association.

The American consul lived in Hamilton Heights, the Stars and Stripes fluttering over immaculate flowerbeds, in a double-storied red brick mansion which Barry Humphries would have immediately identified as Mock Tudor, designed in the days when children's nursemaids lived in a little room off the kitchen.

The ice-maidens had also expounded on Margaret Mead and, like Samoa, the entire house was permeated with an exotic smell – Mansion House coffee, of which there was a mountain in the cellar alongside cans of Dole pineapple, Del Monte and Jolly Green Giant peas, Crisco, and bottles of S&W mayonnaise and ketchup, all my old friends from the *American Woman's Home Companion*.

The Carsons' previous posting had been Lisbon, where the

two little boys, Winston and Charlie, had been born, so in darkest Brisbane the coffee mountain seemed perfectly understandable. Besides, it was hard to imagine Mrs Carson, an ardent Christian Scientist who looked like Grace Kelly, frequenting the Old Vienna. She was pregnant and mostly kept to her bedroom, reading the Bible and drinking Coca-Cola, and when Mr Carson was at home he spent a lot of time strumming his guitar in the den. He favoured *fado*, but every so often it'd be 'Charlie, get your crochet, honey, and come sit with me', whereupon the plangent chords would stop, or I'd actually see him going up the stairs with a resigned look.

One night when he was still at the office and Mrs Carson already asleep, two large purposeful men in suits arrived and made themselves very much at home. 'Where's Charlie keep his whisky?' they said, so I smartly brought them some. If it hadn't been for the visiting Karitane nurse, obviously unacquainted with movies, I'd have been out the back door like greased lightning.

And pretty soon it *is* a movie, not Humphrey Bogart but *Gone With the Wind* gone wrong, because Mrs Carson goes into labour and next thing they're carrying her down the stairs kicking and screaming, blonde hair all dishevelled. It's the first we've heard that going to hospital is against her religious principles.

A few months later, on 19 April 1954 the whole country sees images of two large men strong-arming another blonde, Mrs Evdokia Petrov, towards some place she doesn't want to go either.[13] And I'll remember what the ice-maidens, or the law students, told me about Karl Marx saying history repeats itself, the first time as tragedy and then as farce, thinking sometimes it can happen the other way around and upwards isn't the only direction, as assumed in the questionnaire which had so outraged Ruth in Orientation Week. I suppose they find the alternative too terrible to think about.

***

Inevitably all manner of dark and dreadful things were soon attributed to Pluto, from the Gestapo, Mussolini's *squadristi* and Moseley's Blackshirts to the kidnapping of the Lindbergh baby, debatably King Kong hauling Fay Wray up the Empire State Building, and by 1953, somewhat grudgingly, cuddly old Uncle Joe, so recently their new best friend. Not that it stopped some of them looking in the bright side and associating Pluto with transformation, a better and wiser world being born from the ashes of the old, a process some argued had already begun back with Franklin and Eleanor Roosevelt, possibly even with Woodrow Wilson but which, like Persephone, had just disappeared for a while.

As yet I knew nothing of all this, but as a child plane-spotter the first thing I'd have asked would have been where a planet had come from, at what speed, and where it might be heading. Checked the form guide, as it were, to see how it had performed last time, whether it had any aberrant tendencies. But I'm now eighteen, focused on more personal transformations.

Occasionally Corinth Carson, possibly while showing me how to make boiled frosting and angel cake, had mentioned the need to guard my virginity, but it was already too late. The horse had bolted, and that turned out to be all rubbish too, what they said about agony and blood. Occasionally *Ideal Marriage* had sounded a cautionary note, but I figured in Holland there probably wasn't enough space for girls to go galloping around destroying their maidenheads.

Clem was a bit older than the other medical students, and more serious, so that could have been a lie too, about clergymen's sons being wilder (nobody yet mentioned rabbis' daughters). He had access to a flat with a double bed, and even bought me the right-size diaphragm and the necessary gloop –

any man who'd produced a condom, a university woman would have rejected him immediately, it was unspeakably working class.

After the baby the Karitane nurse moved in full time at the Carsons', so it was back to Arden, the residential in Spring Hill. It was still full of people leading lives of quiet desperation, spinsters and widows who went to business, wearing 'costumes', and men who lay on their beds all day in their underwear, smoking Kensitas and reading the sports pages. The nearest thing to a foreigner was a cheeky Cockney actor who occasionally worked as a gorilla, capering outside cinemas showing King Kong films.

The first time I'd lived at Arden, on evenings when I developed second thoughts about whichever Arts-Law boy I'd said I'd go out with, I'd hide downstairs in the laundry until he gave up knocking on my door and it was safe to go back. But for some reason I'd turned against Clem (wrong colour trousers, wrong shoes?) even though he'd given me a book of Judith Wright poems, and by now the person living next door to the laundry wasn't the gorilla man, but Umberto, an Italian who didn't smoke, knew nothing of football and looked absolutely marvellous in his underwear.

Umberto drove a taxi, and even when he wasn't he never got drunk, and his gold crucifix looked wonderful too against his olive skin with the fine dusting of golden hair. And no risk either he'd go off and marry one of the ice-maidens, when he already had a wife back in Trieste, the mother of his daughter, Algemare.

It meant seaweed, he told me, while I stroked the scar on his thigh. He said it was when he'd been holed up with the partisans in the mountains and been captured by Fascists who'd strung him up to a tree for target practice, and why would I disbelieve him? We'd all grown up reading about such things, and hearing quite ordinary men recount the dangers they had passed.

He couldn't have been lying about the vasectomy either.

***

[11] Theodoor Hendrik van de Velde's *Ideal Marriage: Its Physiology and Technique*, William Heinemann (Medical Books). London, 1940, was reprinted forty-six times and after WW2 sold more than half a million copies.

[12] Two families intensively studied to support arguments for eugenics.

[13] On 11 April, 1954, in Sydney following the defection of her husband, the KGB escorted Mrs Evdokia Petrov to a plane bound for Darwin, where PM Robert Menzies organised for her to be snatched back by ASIO and offered asylum.

Chapter 6
Journalism: *The Courier-Mail and The Longreach Leader*

The next step up from the Shingle Inn, after girls outgrew waffles with caramel syrup and got over being in love with horses, was a café across the street called Rowe's, where Brisbane's upper and middle *Weiberbund* orchestrated their children's weddings. So the preliminary tactical moves may well have been discussed there too, like getting their daughters a job in the *Courier-Mail's* social department.

Denny Lawton swore it wasn't how *she'd* got there, but I didn't know that until 1991, when she organised the first reunion of the Class of '51, all I remembered was the shock horror when she'd left to marry a Catholic and start having seven children.

Even so, any lawyer would have trumped my-son-the-journalist, which I'm pretty sure didn't happen through fathers and uncles playing golf with the publisher, or exchanging Masonic handshakes. More likely it was drinking with the sports editor, and the closest my father had ever got to journalism was knowing Nell Tritton, the daughter of the people responsible for our furniture. Exactly how he never said, though I promptly imagined Nell as another racy socialite like his cousin Eve Mocatta, before she'd gone overseas and married Kerensky, a Commo who wasn't quite as bad as the others.

So why the *Courier-Mail* didn't choose yet another boy for the General Reporters' room, who knows? All I can think is that Queenslanders, less industrialised and closer to the natural world, still understood that every so often there'd be a goat who preferred to mingle with sheep, a snowy dove happier trooping among crows, or a girl disinclined to write about tulle and organza and who bought presents for whom. Or maybe they'd heeded whoever it was, H L Mencken? Ben Hecht? who'd said every good newspaper needed one drunk, one Jew and one Commie, and were adapting it to Australian conditions – a year later they hired Zell Rabin, and there was already one teetotaller, Grace Garlick whose parents were Salvation Army.

What newspapers certainly didn't need was cadets corrupted by university, so it definitely helped that by the end of 1953 I knew I'd failed Accountancy again, and would lose the Commonwealth Scholarship, so walking out of the Psychology 11 exam wouldn't matter. Whoever it was who interviewed me laughed, saying he couldn't imagine it either, me being a public servant in Canberra, though I sensed he wasn't seeing it from my perspective, that I'd be paid two-thirds of whatever men were paid, and have to resign the minute I became engaged.

Grace Garlick had her own desk down in the back corner, but cadets started out at the four desks wedged together outside the Chief of Staff's window, handy to whoever was doing Police Rounds, to acquaint them with the real world. The next highest priority was accuracy, so every cadet also did a stint on radio programs, shipping lists and watering times when householders were permitted to use lawn sprinklers and not get fined.

Naturally the boys had escaped shorthand, so there were three lessons a week in the subs' room around lunchtime, the calm before the storm when the sub-editors were just starting to trickle in, unwrapping brown paper bags of sandwiches, or dribbling ash down their hand-knitted cardigans while they did crossword puzzles. Only later would adrenalin surge and presses thunder as they bellowed through the ever-thickening fug for whichever cadet needed reminding that in the *Courier-Mail*, people didn't reside, purchase, enter into happy nuptial bliss, pass away or have bellybuttons. They lived, bought, married and died and had navels.

Such terms weren't even permissible in reported speech – usually that of a woman with immaculately corrugated hair who, if she permitted me to cross her pristine doorstep, would flick invisible dust from whichever bit of the three-piece lounge suite I was allowed to sit on before being told that ninety percent of whatever I wanted to know was quite *unnecessary*. Satan found work for idle hands to do, all right, the number of things which were unnecessary. If women like that had their way people wouldn't even have had navels.

The chief sub-editor was Clem Astley, father of Thea the future novelist, but when Clem wanted to see you, it wasn't for chats about Australian literature. 'The *Courier-Mail* is a family newspaper, Miss Smith!' But Clem usually had a mean twinkle in his eye, same as the other subs, there wasn't one my father wouldn't have shouted a beer for confirming his worst suspicions, while agreeing it took all sorts to make a world. The big shock horror at the time was customs officers finding the conductor, Sir Eugene Goossens, in possession of 'prohibited articles', possibly the type used by painter Rosaleen Norton, of Kings Cross, who was rumoured to indulge in unnatural sexual practices with a poet called Gavin Greenlees.[14] If Percy Grainger hadn't been living in America, the sub-editors would have bought him a beer too, regardless of his sexual practices, for defending the Anglo-Saxon language.

The *Courier-Mail* wasn't averse to reporters with a sense of the ridiculous, either, so it's ironic that this was the cause of my downfall, though the official version was I'd made one mistake too many with the shipping lists. Even when he's an authority figure, to a girl rising twenty there's something inherently risible about being propositioned by a man old enough to be her grandfather, and shorter than she is.

***

The first-year cadets were paid six pounds a week, but it wasn't until later that I realised the even better thing about journalism was that, except for situations like the above, it gave women some control over men.

In those long-ago days, being faced with a reporter was like Dr Johnson said regarding a man who knows he's to be hanged in a fortnight, it focusses his mind wonderfully. How closely men paid attention, how impeccably they'd behave, never once telling me I talked too much and lapsing into some unintelligible language probably related to football which I suspected would presage something nasty, brutish and short. So I was soon persuaded that God moved in a mysterious way, even if some people had concluded he was taking so long about it he couldn't be really trying, or had never even started. I was being spared what other women were putting up with, saved from the jaws of feminism.

The downside was that the male cadets all lived at home, and the solution to starvation presented itself in an entirely straightforward way, in another coffee shop in Edward Street, the Colony Club. It was Deco-ish with brown wooden booths, frequented by men who understood space, layouts, design and artwork, and knew actual artists like John Rigby, whom they'd heard needed a model for his Tuesday night life class. He was art director at Noble Bartlett's, a leading advertising agency, and the class was in the basement of St Mary's church hall, Kangaroo Point, which also sounded reassuring.

It wasn't a case of shutting my eyes and thinking of England, as Victorian brides were once advised. It was the money, twelve shillings and sixpence an hour times two and once I'd taken off my glasses as well, I couldn't see more than a foot in front of me, much less the dozen or so people seeing me. Besides, as my Colony Club friends explained, they weren't really seeing *me*, just a challenging arrangement of curves and hollows, planes and shadows, and in winter the interesting red flush across whichever bit of me was nearest the single-bar radiator.

This arrangement lasted a couple of years, no longer having to walk home through the back streets of Spring Hill to avoid the smell of the meat and onions sizzling on the greasy hotplate at Ray's and Mae's, the local hamburger shop. But the more feline satisfaction of lying in my foggy world thinking of nothing in particular ended much earlier when John Rigby, due to the pressures of his day job, bequeathed his class to Jon Molvig, whom I now thought about constantly, wishing I wasn't blind and hoping he was, to my physical imperfections.

Molvig was bronzed and bearded, a Viking van Gogh burdened with some secret sorrow I never got to the bottom of, but didn't seem connected to the melon-shaped hole in his ribs I'd briefly felt one night, before he thought better of it and walked me home as usual, over the Storey Bridge, up Fortitude Valley through mean streets filled with brothels, to lash out at Ray's and Mae's. Yet not a single memory remained of what he talked about, so maybe my mind was still elsewhere, hoping he'd reconsider.

Solvency also meant going more often to the Old Vienna, where Igor Wollner, and more especially Magda, were always ready to sit down with anyone in need of solace about the past or encouragement for the future – young persons intent on broadening their horizons by saving up to go to Europe on the *Fairsky*, or reading books that weren't by Ernest Hemingway or John Steinbeck. So naturally that was where I'd gone shortly after I was fired, but instead of offering encouragement about my imminent job interview, Magda reached across our coffees and strudel and undid an extra two buttons of my cardigan, a truly startling gesture as it was a cold day and every other woman I knew would have buttoned it up completely.

My only other mentor in the feminine arts was Mrs Palfreyman, an elegant brunette war widow on the Elizabeth Arden counter in Allan and Stark's department store who hired me to clean her pretty house once a week. But her advice was the mere foothills compared with the message I was getting now from Magda, or rather its subtext. Life wasn't like *Pride and Prejudice,* Mrs Bennet confident of a thunderstorm and sending Jane off lightly clad to Netherleigh, the better to ensnare Mr Bingley. To be truly European and civilised, a girl had to look seductive around the clock, rain or shine, in sickness or in health, regardless of what she, or any men she met, might be intending. When in my recent experience, men needed no encouragement whatsoever.

***

The good man everyone went to was another Viennese, but that was definitely something I couldn't ask Magda about, after Umberto went to Darwin and was replaced by an ABC producer who lent me copies of Theatre Arts and hadn't had a vasectomy. Still, the entry in the medical directory was reassuring, and there wasn't a file on him in the *Courier-Mail's* clippings library, though obviously he was there in the broader generic sense, under Migrants, European.

One thing I knew about from the Old Vienna was golf balls, how hard it was to stuff in those long squiggly rubber strips, but for medical men it was usually worse, years working as wardsmen in places like Georgetown with no going home at night to play Schubert quartets and chess with old friends, let alone a nubile widow of the same religion. So it all turned out far better than it might have if I'd got some doctor accustomed to deferential worship like the one at University (my first encounter with a male doctor) who'd checked me out to be certain I hadn't had TB, and possibly for syphilis too, as the more worldly students had whispered about something called a Wasserman test.

We even had a chat about Heine while he was putting my legs in the stirrups, at the house in New Farm with the jacaranda trees. Or was it while he was driving me home in his grey Jag, concerned there'd be nobody to take care of me?

***

Around this time I'd occasionally be told by world-weary men that the character of nations, at least in the New World, was determined by the time of their birth, the *zeitgeist,* that because the United States had been born in 1776, Americans had never got over liberty, all very well (though perhaps the right to bear arms had gone too far), whereas Australia's birth, as a country rather than an offshore jail, had been in the nineteenth century, attuning us to nobler things like equality and workers' rights. Why, look at South Africa, over there they've never got beyond apartheid because it was settled by Dutch Calvinists back in ... well, never mind. Before the Enlightenment, anyway.

At the time I assumed they'd understood synchronicity, Jung's theory of the collective unconscious, though later I figured it was more likely they'd read Alexis de Tocqueville, that there was virtually nothing which couldn't be explained by the point of departure.[15] But if you were unwise enough to let them buy you another beer, all you'd hear about would be the English Chartist movement and trade unions, when what I'd have liked to be enlightened about was why individual *people* were the way they were, even if they'd never heard how they were supposed to be. Did time and space make a difference, influence what ultimately happened to them?

For instance Cousin Ollie, dear old Mina's son, who'd seemed destined to be a schoolteacher. If anyone in our family was going to win the annual Queensland concerto competition playing the Rach One or Rach Three, whichever is the more horrendously difficult, we'd have predicted it'd be Cousin Billy. But it was how Aquarians were supposed to be, liable to do shocking things, like Denny Lawton who could have been contender herself if she hadn't married the Catholic lawyer.

At University, despite the *Gnothi Seauton* inscribed above another flight of sandstone steps further along from the one where the cashmere virgins congregated, knowing oneself, or ascertaining what the universe might have in store for you, had been another either/or thing like nature versus nurture or freewill versus fate, already shrunken to one malevolent entity whereas in my uncles' art books it took at least three Fates, Clotho, Lachesis and Atropos exercising considerable judgment, and two goddesses, Tyche and Nemesis, representing luck and divine retribution. Time and place, which year and which side of the hill, now only affected grapes.

Today it's so easy, one click and you can discover what de Tocqueville himself may well have noticed by 1846, that the main reason Le Verrier lost out was the German astronomer Friedrich von Struve pointing out that Neptune was the only Olympian god without a planet named after him. Jupiter had one, Saturn had one, it wasn't fair. Equality was already triumphing, just as de Tocqueville feared.

Luckily Neptune was quite a nice old thing, something like a marine Santa Claus, no previous form for child-devouring, spouse abuse or changing women into heifers, only occasional dalliance with mermaids. (Though Seneca said he had a wife, Salacia, the goddess of salt water). But the Greeks and Romans were thinking of the mild Mediterranean, not oceans with tsunamis, Sargasso Seas, giant squids and great white whales, or Coleridge's mast-high icebergs as green as emerald. And by the 1840s the burgeoning Western middle classes wanted things to stay that way. *Nice.* No more nasty revolutions (though some found them rather thrilling) and a misty veil drawn over any unpleasantness.

That's a sea god's job, to dissolve reality by facilitating altered states of consciousness, whether through artistic inspiration, suspension of rational disbelief, or just plain old alcohol and opium. But it's a fine line, a permeable membrane, that separates illusion from delusion, and before long it's more than just Turner and Caspar David Friedrich landscapes, Sir Walter Scott and the invention of painless dentistry. The Enlightenment goal, to ascertain how things work, and how much, if any, change was possible or desirable, is already succumbing to the urge to save and rescue – today fallen women and inebriates, tomorrow the world! Has not Schiller already dreamt that one day all men will be brothers?

Again, most people agree this would still have happened if Neptune had been called Le Verrier, though some might argue that if eleven-year-old girls had had any say, it would have been called Orpheus, after the musician who turns back to rescue his beloved from the underworld. Or better still, Eurydice – as by now girls have surely heard of *The Vindication of the Rights of Women.* But what's Mary Wollstonecraft compared with Neptune, the god of horses? The luckiest Eurydice ever gets is fifteen seconds of fame in 1862, thanks to a C H F Peters who'd just discovered an M-type spectrum asteroid.

***

The job on *The Longreach Leader* required quite a bit of deception, like claiming I was twenty-one, already a graded journalist and had left the *Courier-Mail* of my own accord. A country paper was always a smart move, my old colleagues said. A year or two's suffering, you'd be able to handle absolutely everything, get back on some decent metropolitan daily with no trouble.

Certainly it was different from being a secretary at Cossey Waite advertising agency, hearing about old movies and being lent amusing books by S J Perelman. Different too from 4KY The Catholic Station, being Girl Friday to George Hardman, a portly announcer everyone knew had been living devotedly in sin for years. But my old mates were absolutely right, especially about the suffering.

Whatever it was in Longreach that earned a girl Brownie points, the way football and mechanical talents had once ensured my father's success in Roma, I never discovered. It was some faint help that not too long ago Uncle Tom, the one who'd married Aunt Madeleine, had managed the ES&A bank. But the people who'd really known them lived far away, not in the town, which as ecosystems go was seriously truncated, more like the two-tier community you get in prisons or asylums – warders, and inmates serving anything from a few months to life – with food to match. Never had I eaten so many tinned peaches, longed so desperately for a fresh lettuce.

Things improved slightly when I moved from the house where the radio was on all day to the Commercial Hotel, home to single bank clerks, passing salesmen, and remittance men. As television hadn't yet happened, there was little to do at night if you didn't fancy drinking, but 1956 was the year of the shearers' strike and most nights, from the upstairs veranda, you could watch a brawl, up to five men kicking another one lying on the pavement and nobody daring to intervene.

Pretty soon there was an actual dead body, in the backyard of some other hotel. You don't forget that either, the rigidity, yellow skin and buzzing flies on what looked like a glassed throat, though it was later ruled to be natural causes. But with the social pages I was the perpetrator, offending and insulting some woman every week by not naming her ahead of some lesser one, or describing her ball gown as magenta instead of fuchsia.

My own two ball gowns were magnificent, created with the help of my Czech dressmaker Francoise, wife of Erik the carpenter. They never went to balls, which were reputed to be major occasions for violence and class warfare, when a man could be taken out the back and beaten up for asking a girl for a dance if she was Town and he was Country, or vice versa. Rex, the ABC man from Sydney, never went either, apart from Keith, an Englishman who sold tractors and introduced me to the Goon Show, nobody I knew went anywhere, because there was no there there that wouldn't have been the same as Longreach only smaller – a dusty main street with goats clambering on cars to nibble on the pepperina trees.

Not that I didn't try, jumping at Keith's invitation to come to Isisford, about seventy-three miles away, for the day, only the car broke down in the vicinity of Portland Downs, one of those properties the size of Belguim. I trudged on for hours in my dainty high-heeled sandals, hoping Keith wasn't dying back under the scrubby tree where he'd collapsed in the February heat, and that mirages didn't happen in outback Queensland.But it was a real shearing shed, with a trough of slimy green water where I sat for quite a while, my hooped petticoat floating around my ears, looking up at the big house on the hill and hoping that was real too.

The owners were away but someone retrieved Keith and drove us, scarcely able to move, to a pub in Isisford where we fell asleep in our own twin beds listening to the Saturday night outdoor movie, *Waterloo Bridge*, the one where Vivien Leigh, an ex-ballerina reduced to prostitution, ends up hurling herself under a bus, which could have been what the townsfolk of Longreach expected too, of girls who'd spent a dirty weekend with some foreigner.

The Longreach Leader itself was brilliant, just me and the editor, Mr Campbell, a small canny Scot with political ambitions, which meant writing even more of it under increasing stress as he kept reminding me to get myself on the electoral roll. But fortunately he knew when a joke had gone far enough, an essential talent in an editor, and shortly before the election he called me in for a drink and told me he'd known from the start I wasn't old enough to vote, and wasn't a graded journalist either. But I was doing fine.

It made me feel better about the persuasive letters I'd been writing to *Woman,* down in Sydney, knowing I hadn't been lying, or not that much, and that if Mr Campbell had known about this too, he'd have given me every encouragement.

***

[14] In 1956, Sir Eugene Goossens was arrested and charged for attempting to bring 800 erotic photographs, some film and ritual masks into Australia. He pleaded guilty, was fined £100, resigned from the Sydney Symphony Orchestra and the NSW Conservatorium and returned to Britain.

[15] Alexis de Tocqueville, *Democracy in America,* University of Chicago Press, 2000, ed & trans Harvey Mansfield & Delba Winthrop. 'There is not one opinion, one habit, one law, I could say one event, that the point of departure does not explain.'

Chapter 7
Woman's Day, Sydney

A travelling salesman's car gets stuck in a snow bank. Hours later, half frozen, he reaches a farmhouse. Can he have a bed?

'Sure', says the farmer, 'but I ain't got no daughter for ya to sleep with, like ya always hear about in them thar jokes'.

'Oh!' said the salesman. 'How far is it to the next house?'

***

In King Street there were wonderful shops, jewellers and furriers – I'd never seen a fur coat before – and fishmongers' windows with water perpetually trickling down on newly-opened rock oysters. And most famously de Luca's with the tropical fruit.

One day I was smelling a pineapple (you never knew what they'd do in Sydney, take them out of cold storage too soon, or dye them yellower) when there was this fraffly refeened voice.

'You'd wonder where some people was brung up'.

The only other person in the shop was a woman in long cyclamen gloves and a fussy cyclamen hat, what my mother would have called all dolled up. But it was a bit surprising even so, because one thing I'd quickly discovered was that in big cities, it's all about *not* seeing things that *are* there. Drunks, funny-peculiar people talking to themselves, even people crying right under their noses on bus-stops, or wanting to talk because they're angry or possibly just plain happy.

As city people said, you didn't want to get involved, though there's no risk yet of being sued for a random act of kindness. But of course I *did,* as there were things I'd never encountered back in Queensland, like taxi drivers with heavy accents who said 'Zo?

Vy exactly should you vant to know?' in a menacing tone when you asked where they came from. However would they have learnt English, or anything else, if *they* hadn't asked questions? And what's the point of horses, if not to give girls the ability to coax large truculent creatures into some semblance of compliance? So I was soon privy to, if not their secret griefs, their grievances and opinions, which paradoxically often coincided with my father's, especially regarding Southerners' aversion to work.

The taxi drivers also had strong political views, and although Sydney people would laughingly insist it was only conservatives who saw Reds under beds, ie things which weren't there, there wasn't a soul whose eyes weren't peeled for germs – one sneeze and they'd be telling you about something that was, or would be, going around, thrusting some nasty-tasting lozenge upon you. Even their famous oysters weren't to be trusted, as they ate a bad one quite often. In fact city people didn't seem to trust anyone, forever demanding receipts, dockets and doctors' certificates, and saying 'sorry!' even when they'd merely brushed against you.

Clearly, trust was the first casualty of urban life, followed by fear that at any moment anyone could catch anything, be fatally struck down. Next thing they'd be telling me the sun rose in the west. And why did they always *fall* pregnant, as in fall from grace, or into error or sin? Religion was at the bottom of it, that was for sure, and possibly the class struggle too.

***

Home was now a converted attic in Berry Street, Neutral Bay, with steeply sloping ceilings and a big front room with a bay window and a padded seat, overlooking the garden with the magnolia tree. There was a famous poet, Rosemary Dobson, living next door, and down the leafy back lane where I'd walk to the bus stop, a writer of children's books, Lorna Ross Williams, who'd sometimes ask me in for coffee.

But with city nights there was no question of mysterious and marvellous changes, boiled tongue in the press becoming jelled by morning, sick animals healing or dying, a hundred chickens doubled in size under their aluminium tent. The Pleiades and Orion's Belt struggled for attention in a petulant sky which ached to be properly black, even the moon you had to be quick about before it disappeared too, like the Russian Sputnik with the whimpering dog inside.

At Berry Street, possums frisked and scampered across the roof, which they'd never done at home. Everyone said they were a curse, weaselling under eaves and peeing in the ceiling, leaving a smell as horrible as when they fell down chimneys and died behind the fireplaces which had been bricked in and replaced by electric heaters in the cause of progress and efficiency.

Possums were one of my first stories at *Woman*, but it seemed that Vaucluse, even leafier than Neutral Bay, had another form of wildlife.

'Silvertailed whats?' I asked.

It had been June when I arrived, men wearing tweedy hats and overcoats. But gloves! How astounded we'd been seeing Americans put them on to change a tyre, we'd thought the only men who wore gloves were polar explorers or pilots. Sheila's husband Hackie, who was somewhere in North Africa, had sent back a pair belonging to a captured German, huge sinister black leather ones with white lambswool lining. My mother had promptly stashed them in a cupboard but I'd get them out every so often, smelling Germany the way I'd smelt India in Chandra Lal's spices.

The *Woman* office had been another surprise, no longer at the city address to which I'd sent my intransigent letters, politely declining their offer to employ me as a secretary. It had moved a few weeks earlier, out of what looked like an incredibly historic building, to Ultimo, which I'd pronounced *Ulteemo*, into a brutish concrete edifice, ten stories at least, just off Broadway, where instead of theatres there were pubs and a pungent brewery, a row of little shops and a cheerful chemist called Phil Goldberg who discreetly obliged the desperate and careless.

All the *Woman* journalists looked dauntingly sophisticated, even those who hadn't been war correspondents, gone off on troopships or interviewed General Macarthur. Joan Reader, Sally Baker, Ailsa Craig, and later Anne Dupree, not one of them didn't look capable of hurling grenades and defying the Japanese to dig another sliver of bamboo under her fingernails. They could also smoke while typing with both hands, a skill I never mastered. 'Anyone got a threepenny bit?' they'd cry, when a suspender button failed. Not since St Margaret's had I seen such insouciant hauling-up of skirts, such revelations of underwear.

There were also revelations on other levels – the existence of husbands, usually shed, or lovers, whose children occasionally dropped by in private school uniforms, and often, too, a warning glance from a third party to indicate some office relationship was more intimate than I'd thought. But like any newcomer I misread a lot of things and went too far.

There was a sofa in the washroom, and not remembering one at the *Courier-Mail,* I assumed it was a concession to the frailty of Southern women in general, a real journalist wouldn't be seen dead on it, or dream of resorting to the in-house doctor – another novelty. So I was amazed to find *Woman* considered mumps a serious illness, something anyone should have vivid memories of, and as I didn't, I was banished for three weeks with assurances that a Doctor Selby, who wrote *Woman's* medical column and lived nearby, would drop by every so often. But I don't recall suffering in the slightest, and mostly he'd just sit on my bed and chat about interesting medical matters, how mumps could make men sterile, and the perils of rubella in early pregnancy.

I was also ignorant of a local custom, that on the first Monday in October NSW banks shut for Labour Day. I'd have died rather than ask anyone to lend me a bus fare and walked all through town, across the famous Bridge, and only burst into tears when I got home. Somehow it was much worse than being lost on Portland Downs, where there'd been people at the other end.

A few months later the kitchen ceiling collapsed in the small hours, chunks of ancient plaster hitting the gas taps of the cooker. My first thought was that my earlier visitor had returned, a former colleague from the *Courier-Mail* who'd stormed down the stairs around midnight, shouting that I was frigid or a lesbian or both, though it hardly seemed to call for my extermination. But Mrs Murch downstairs said it was just one of those things that happened with old houses.

At home too there'd been acts of God, but in Sydney people were confident of bringing them under control, and should the best efforts of medical science prove futile, they'd persuade themselves it was actually a blessing in disguise. Every morning I'd pray, please God, don't let them give me a two-headed baby story. No brave kiddies in iron lungs.

Luckily my prayers were answered. For this kind of story, anything seriously heart-wrenching and morally instructive, they always sent a mother.

***

Wal, though ten years old than me, wasn't like the world-weary journalists, with their *zeitgeists* and what passes for a political conversation in Australia, why Labor deserved to win or hadn't deserved to lose. He was a photographer and his view was closer to my father's and mine, both sides were equally bad only in different ways. It was a couple of months until we met because he'd been in hospital with pneumonia, which accounted for the ox-blood and ginger-checked dressing gown that so appalled me a few months later when he moved in. The sort worn by decrepit old men sunning themselves on the verandas of workers' cottages, and later by Barry Humphries when he's being Sandy Stone.

His mother had bought it for him at Gowings, Wal told me, with an eloquent shrug to make it clear that *he'd* never have set foot there, if he'd had any say, not been close to fucking death, it would have been something silky, burgundy or a discreet paisley, more George Raftish and free from some place which owed *Woman* a favour.

Oh, he was cynical all right, just like the newspaper heroes in the movies, right down to his moustache and slicked-back dark hair. A man who'd been down mean streets (I hadn't yet discovered that he himself was not unmean), who hadn't just seen the movies but read the books too. Raymond Chandler, Fitzgerald, Budd Schulberg, S J Perelman.

Hadn't those advertising men back in Brisbane, the ones who explained 'crazy like a fox' meant extra smart, told me he'd written the Marx Brothers films? Christ, didn't I know *anything*?

Wal had been working for Fairfax since he'd left school, so it stood to reason some woman had snapped him up ages ago, probably some mousy typist who'd never heard of Perelman, or verisimilitude, until he'd told her.[16] Besides, *Woman* was forever sending us off together on assignments, and Wal being the sort of man women of a certain age tend to indulge, I figured if he'd been single they'd have done the exact opposite, tried to keep him away from any nubile interlopers.

It was Wal who told me about being as conspicuous as a tarantula on a piece of angel cake, who laughed with me about the Goon Show – he did a mean Gritpype Fynne, even looked like

Peter Sellers – and recalled *Scoop* in hotel lounges while we waited for our quarry to emerge. So we soon fell into that easy familiarity which makes people assume you're a married couple.

In Sydney, unlike Brisbane, there were never any rebuffs on doorsteps. What was there to fear from *Woman?* Besides, it was often in the Eastern Suburbs where, now that he'd enlightened me about the silvertails, I felt secure enough to reveal the existence of Aunt Trudie and her daughter Mary in Darling Point. But whenever we ventured further afield, he'd teach me further cheerful facts about social geography, the art of predicting where we could expect plaster ducks flying up the walls, a cuppa instead of a gin and tonic from a genuine antique sideboard as opposed to a cocktail bar with padded vinyl stools and kitschy mottoes. Home-made scones rather than *gugelhopf.* (It seemed my father had been right about 'Double Pay' and 'Belljew Hill'.)

Because photographers need to slope off for a quick recce to find the perfect location, and fiddle with blinds and curtains, Wal's special expertise was refrigerators, the contents of which would confirm everything a foxy woman should have suspected the minute she reached the front gate. Far better than bookshelve - if there were any, or the books weren't just artful reproductions, like we'd seen at some politician's place.

As with the Three Bears' beds and porridge, with refrigerators there was a happy medium. Not too full, indicating the owners still feared crop failure or imminent transportation, yet not too empty either, as often happened with a) people whose minds were on higher things, cultural or academic pursuits, or b) people who were just plain skint and keeping up appearances. I wouldn't believe, Wal said, how many refrigerators there were in desirable North Shore residences with nothing but a cracked Royal Doulton egg-cup of fossilised mustard, the dangerously ancient remains of a meat loaf, and a bunch of soggy celery. Old

Money that had run out, he explained, or where they'd been used to servants.

The Western Suburbs had lots of groaning refrigerators too, Wal told me, but we almost never went further than Ashfield, usually to some nice Federation house like the one his paternal grandparents had lived in before they'd moved to a grander one in Chatswood. The sea captain who'd bought the bond store in the Rocks which now belonged to someone else, that he'd pointed out to me once when we were driving over the Harbour Bridge, a smokestack saying Rowan's Bond.

When Wal first assessed my refrigerator, I'd been confident his diagnosis would be thrifty farmer's daughter, or slightly distressed landed gentry. But no. Despite Bea Miles, a wellborn but malodorous eccentric, jumping into my taxi one day and reciting Shakespeare, an experience I'd been led to believe made one a true Sydneysider, I wasn't. In Wal's eyes, and perhaps everyone else's, I was one of those hillbillies from Psychology 1, Daisy Mae from Dogpatch, Kentucky - another Miss Independent Front Suspension - in the *L'il Abner* comic strip. I should have known, the first joke he'd ever told me was the one about the farmer's daughter who agrees to have it off with six men and a bear and afterwards asks who was that foreigner in the fur coat? Though paradoxically we were considered world champions at knowing bullshit when we saw it.

But Wal had seemed confident I could assimilate, that the country could be taken out of the girl, and forgave me the absence of salami and pickles (taboo since my schoolgirl forays into the health food store), as I would later forgive him the anaphrodisical dressing gown, and eventually the revelations about his father whose long absence overseas on a business trip had always quivered in the background. Not that I was told half of it, but enough for a girl to be getting on with on the night before her wedding.

I should have known it was more than the hard-boiled movie heroes, that people don't get that way without a good reason. Cynical and amusing, adept at verisimilitude.

***

As I've said, with Australian men there was generally a language problem sooner or later, but when propinquity led to what they then called promiscuity I'd immediately known what Wal meant, as he wasn't remotely interested in sport. Possibly *Woman* knew too, because I'd been transferred to Fiction, as assistant to the editor, Mrs Gwen Beaumont, who wasn't at all the war-correspondent type.

My days were now entirely sedentary, yet still filled with intellectual challenge, staying eternally vigilant for a tintack, a weenie, an elevator, a train station or a zit requiring translation. Sometimes I was entrusted with an entire relocation, from Nantucket to Surfers, or Gross Pointe to Vaucluse. But it was always Mrs Beaumont who dealt with the moral lapses, girls who went too far and got hickeys.

These rarely happened, the authors were too well-trained. The only slow learners were publishers, who sent us review copies of just about everything except books on popular mechanics – by 1956 Australian women were over the thrill of changing tyres and fixing broken axles, as the Queen had famously done in her Princess Elizabeth days. But particularly books on what clergymen in Sydney, even Church of England ones, referred to as 'the occult'.

The Sisters of the Sacred Advent, even the Sunday morning sermons at St John's, had never mentioned the occult, much less ouija boards, which it seemed were even more perilous than alcohol. Working with godless journalists, it took me a while to realise that in Sydney the Church of England was Low, closer to

Methodists, and conclude that must have been the reason - with clergymen like Dean Baddeley, going to the races in his cassock, backing winners and wanting cinemas to open on Sundays, it never occurs to you to become an atheist.

I'd never have dared call Mrs Beaumont Gwen, but occasionally she'd mention her Celtic heritage and tell me more about the sky I'd once looked at with my mother, the level beyond the cirrus and cumulo-nimbus clouds of our plane-spotting days. Much of it I already knew, that unlike Aquarians I cared deeply about food and material comforts, and that Wal was technically gifted and hyper-critical, but it was Mrs Beaumont who taught me to see there was much more to it, that the world-weary drinkers were onto something, and there was some purpose to maths and geometry.

If only my father had known about the occult, instead of cricket balls, slower and faster trains, and accelerating cheetahs!

***

We got married at the Sydney Registry Office. If I ever hoped to pass successfully, cease being Daisy Mae from Dogpatch, I had to pretend tradition was all rubbish. In 1950s Australia it was a bit too early for the idea that marriage itself was rubbish, and who needed a piece of paper – another paradox, given their preference for the visible and the tangible. Not that I'm saying it there aren't times when it could be important, like when we were signing the register and I noticed my mother-in-law was born Esther Symonds.

'Was your mother Jewish?' It might explain why he looked like Peter Sellers.

'Don't be fucking *ridiculous*'.

I let it ride, being a little sensitive by now about my own name, its association with dirty weekends and, far less amusingly, George Orwell's *1984*. Why couldn't it have been Winston *Brown*

84

who was nibbled by rats, heard clocks striking thirteen and worried about the boot stamping on a human face forever?

***

[16] A favourite Perelman word from W S Gilbert, *The Mikado*, 'Merely corroborative detail, intended to give artistic verisimilitude to an otherwise bald and unconvincing narrative.'

Chapter 8
An Unnatural Wife and Mother

'It's because they've seen you in a moment of weakness,' he explains, parking the car in some spot I'd never have dared.

It's now about five years into my marriage, and today we're not in the Mercedes but the sports car with the amusing number plate, off to a restaurant where he'll introduce me to New York cuts, or some pâté which won't be as good as the last one he had in Paris or at the Savoy. Complain yet again how it's impossible to buy fresh limes in Australia. Defy Yahweh with chilli prawns.

'Because prawns and lobsters feed around estuaries, on all sorts of rubbish.'

'So that accounts for not eating oysters either?'

'You're so smart, why aren't you rich?'

Nor is he impressed that we Smiths once performed a few miracles (who's he think was going to turn those swords into ploughshares?). Because *his* family goes back to God, not that it isn't a miracle to find someone in Australia who's comfortable with genealogy.

But regarding Max's own moments of weakness, the back story to the midnight knock on the door in Vienna, I discover little. Just enough to make me appreciate how smart his family were to get out before it got worse, and for him to be even smarter, which I've seen already – the thrusting apartment blocks, the Havana cigars and welcoming maitre-d's. Never being reduced to stuffing golf balls (*toi toi toi* and three raps on the table), and always happy to enlighten me about their Enlightenment, the *Haskalah*, how lucky they were not to wind up with some insulting name like Strauss or Schnabel. Though for some, fate could strike later.

A Jew arrives at Ellis Island, knowing he must forget everything about life in the old country.

'Name?' says the immigration man.

'*Schon vergessen*' he replies. And is officially renamed Sean Ferguson.

But when Max explains why I don't much like the women who were there the night I fainted in the pub, that's what I'm really looking for, more than the sex or the Margaritas. The superior insight of people who really know about weakness and keeping up appearances.

Like the fresh limes, insight had been surprisingly hard to come by from people who were supposed to know, considering the former war correspondents had immediately known the primary reason I'd fainted, if not the secondary one, that Wal had just told me he'd had a little talk with Phil the chemist who knew a reliable man.

Only boyfriends did things like that, not husbands.

***

I'd assumed being married would mean going overseas sooner, we'd hitchhike around Europe and I'd perfect my French and German while we picked grapes or assembled Volkswagens. Two could live as cheap as one, *Fifty Exciting Ways with Mince!* like the cookery captions said.

But Wal had been sadly corrupted by journalism. To afford a car and stay in hotels we'd need to save some impossibly large sum, meaning I'd be thirty, maybe thirty-five, before I could think about a baby. Why else had we got married? It wasn't just to have sex, which we'd been having already. And soon there wasn't even that.

Around my sixth month *Woman's Day,* as it had then become, held a little farewell ceremony and presented me with a blue blanket. I could never go back, Fairfax wouldn't have married couples in the same office, and working for the opposition, *Women's Weekly*, was out of question. Still, my brilliant career wasn't quite over at twenty-three, as they arranged for me to do a little work at home, selecting readers' letters for publication.

Only one woman had ever come back, Helen Gordon who'd unblushingly stayed pregnant to Roley Moody, a sub-editor on *The Daily Telegraph* old enough to be her father. She'd returned lithe and soignée, with cropped black hair, looking like I imagined Frenchwomen on the Rive Gauche, and not in the least depressed.

That was another of their strange beliefs, as one of the first things I'd been taught was that the only creature that isn't more afraid of you than you are of it is anything newly-maternal, from magpies to cows, especially Jerseys.

I hung out quite a bit at their place at Newport, watching Helen, cigarette jammed in the corner of her mouth, nonchalantly changing nappies and dealing with sundry disasters. 'Worse things have happened at sea', she'd say. She knew whereof she spoke, as *Woman's Day* had gone through a phase of having her spend a day on a submarine, or in a helicopter, a dying flicker of *nostalgie de la guerre.* So I was determined to emulate her, while wondering whatever she saw in Roley. The way she'd drive off around midnight to collect him from work, and stay up till dawn helping him drink red wine while he expounded on the Spanish Civil War. Or maybe it was the October Revolution.

Even if I hadn't been pregnant, with politics I'd always follow what Wal said was time-honoured journalist practice, I made an excuse and left, seeing that's what it always was. Left. By this time I was thinking surely Tolstoy couldn't be right, one thing every unhappy family probably had in common would be that the wife wouldn't much care about whatever hostilities had happened, or were about to happen, in the wider world.

But later it seemed it was just me who'd been oblivious to everything either side of JFK being assassinated (vacuuming the carpet, which I'd dyed purple to hide the stains of cheap flagon red), except for English model Jean Shrimpton scandalising Melbourne racegoers in 1965 by attending the Derby hatless and gloveless and Mandy Rice-Davies inventing, admittedly inadvertently, that invaluable test of newsworthiness, 'well, he would, wouldn't he?' So as every other formerly-unhappy woman seems to have total recall of world events in this period, either they weren't all that unhappy or they were living with someone like Roley, not that the one would necessarily preclude the other. [17]

Anyway, it was great when people started saying if you could remember the Sixties, you couldn't have really been there.

***

One thing the *Courier-Mail* had always made perfectly clear to cadets, early and often, was that everything we wrote would be next week's fish and chip wrappers, never that it might trigger socio-political transformation from the very first word – *J'accuse*!

I'd figured the other cadets, being boys, mightn't have been exposed to too much history, but quite old journalists, thirty going on sixty, who must surely have heard of Emile Zola and Drefyus, told us exactly the same. [18] So we all believed we should remain cool-headed observers and that the next step, should we attempt writing novels, would be growing the splinter of ice in the heart.

That must have been what was forming in there after I got married, though later it felt more like the splinters of glass I was increasingly having to having to pick out of the formerly-beige shag carpet.

One thing Sydney did better was spring, which in 1958 was having a trial run on the first of August, the morning after I'd become an adulteress. He'd come around to show me how to write scripts for the ABC children's program, and I was not walking, but floating down the street past the white jasmine spilling its heart out, and my own heart like a singing bird, aware of the baby exulting too, with a merry squirm like a tiny electric eel. There were normal husbands after all!

How he'd marvelled at my massive belly, and my blue-veined breasts which were bigger too than when he'd last seen them. Wonderful, like ripe peaches, almost mystical! He wouldn't have minded another kid himself, but she'd said two were enough.

By the time I was pregnant again, my mother had come to the rescue, selling up at Caloundra, and we'd moved into the back half of what was technically our own place, a lovely old Federation house in Cremorne. The bank manager had tried to tell us it was a decaying suburb, but I'd agreed with Wal. Allambie fucking *Heights*? Miles from fucking *nowhere*?

The back room, a sleep-out tacked on after the war, now contained my desk at one end and the washing machine at the other, across an expanse of seagrass matting. It overlooked the back garden with the lemon tree and the big camphor laurels, and what I did there was called 'typing'. Admittedly this had begun as a joke, Truman Capote being dismissive about Jack Kerouac, but it hadn't been long before it came to mean an indulgence best finished soon.[19]

After the readers' letters, I'd moved on to writing the wedding page for the *North Shore Times*, which meant occasional accusations regarding Charles Morgan who delivered the photographs on Wednesday afternoons. But it wasn't until I started freelancing for *The Bulletin* that the real trouble started.

It involved going out to work, then a mortal sin for Australian mothers, and in Wal's eyes, far worse. As Imam Hilali would say, sixty years on, I was like uncovered meat to cats.[20]

Real Australian men didn't yet write about culture, so at *The Bulletin* the fearsomely literate Pat Rolfe, B.A Hons, Sydney, snaffled the writers, leaving me with the artists. 'Like pulling teeth,' she'd say. It made sense, unlike a lot of things Pat said with the same faint smile, expecting me to know already, or possibly not. Who the hell was Pooter? [21] I suspected Prufrock was somebody in T S Eliot, (the ice-maidens had enthused about *The Waste Land,* so I'd never read him) and knew Jacobean and Carolingian poets meant in the time of the Stuart kings, the Jameses and Charles, but surely only Sweden had had kings called Augustus? [22]

Anyway, Pat was right about the artists, especially Jon Molvig. She'd said he was notoriously uncommunicative, and called my story *Enigma Without Variations: the Silences of Jon Molvig,* so I concluded he'd probably been largely silent, too, on our walks home in the 1950s, not that by now my mind wasn't still elsewhere, thinking if I'd gone to Brisbane Tech, like Molvig, instead of university, I might have met a nice ex-serviceman who didn't wear drip-dry nylon shirts and already have a wife. Perhaps Pat had even mentioned Marina Tsvetaeva or Anna Akhmatova, and I'd pretended that I'd known about her too, whichever one wrote that some other woman was leading her life.

As compensation for the artists, Pat would assign me the colourful personalities, American celebrities like Pete Seeger and Roger Miller, dotty aristocrats and iffy lords, (Edith Sitwell, Lord Montague of Beaulieu) and the local equivalent – mostly radio personalities, John Laws, Bob Rogers, and the formidable Andrea at 2UE, at her apartment in the splendidly Art Deco Macleay

Regis ('*Free from Bunions, Husbands and Regrets*'). But after meeting Max, increasingly longer periods of 'typing' were devoted to creativity, and Wal became amazing good at housework. He even cleaned things which were clean already, or clean enough, noisily scouring and scrubbing for hours so he could thrust his reddened puffy hands at me.

J'accuse!

There were only three grounds for divorcing a husband. Insanity – Wal and his mother sometimes visited his father, who'd been diagnosed as hypomanic, which I gathered meant late-onset shellshock. Adultery, I'd thought all men succumbed sooner or later. But one who refused to retaliate, even on suspicion, was like people who didn't get back on a horse or punch playground bullies. Shameful. The third ground was desertion, fat chance. As I've said, Wal was the kind of man older women indulged, and my mother was no exception.

But drinking? You'd have to be joking, love, said the first two lawyers I consulted, an Irishman and a Jew (respectable firms didn't do divorce). The third one, Ted, thought cruelty might be a goer, but there'd have to be visible and tangible evidence, meaning me getting punched, and not the inflatable Esso tiger, for at least six weeks, preferably months. And even if I'd had busted teeth and purple contusions, I didn't know how to take photographs. Not that I hadn't shown an interest.

'I'll take the pictures. You shut up and write!'

The psychotherapist in Mosman said it was scientifically proven that women who married alcoholics secretly wanted to reform them. Well, she would, wouldn't she? Psychotherapists trained in the States where they'd had Prohibition, so Faulkner was definitely right, over there the past wasn't over, it wasn't even past, not if Americans were still drinking ice water with meals. In Australia, how could a woman be expected to tell?

The marriage guidance counsellor, the North Shore dentist's wife, I only went to because Wal was already going and Ted said it'd be evidence of good intent. In her opinion, alcoholism was caused by bad wives.

Wal had always photographed the cookery pages and after Margaret Fulton arrived he'd come home with recipes and little foil-covered containers – a delectable fish pie with anchovies, the recipe alas long gone, *boeuf bourguignon* or *coq au vin,* which I was allowed to make when people came to dinner. They rarely did, mostly it was Helen and John, the brother of Judith the actress Wal had been engaged to until she'd gone to Melbourne for *Hellzapoppin* and sent a telegram saying she was going to marry the already famous John Bluthal.

The elegant maternity dress I'd created didn't count either, cream furnishing fabric patterned with big medallions of pink and green roses, with a scoop neckline edged in pale green satin to match the buttons. Neither did my charitable acts, bequeathing it to Verna, wife of *Bulletin* editor Peter Coleman, where it'd be nice to think it exerted some prenatal influence as the baby is now the writer, Ursula Dubosarsky.

If only Mrs Easton were not constantly *out!*

I'd been a casual on *TV Times* but the ABC didn't employ married women.[23] So now I was writing the daily television pages for *The Sun,* hoping it'd lead to a proper staff job so I could leave and take the kids.

If only Mrs Easton had more women friends! *Naice* ones.

I had a few friends, mostly single, from university days, but it seemed they were all pseudo-intellectual lesbians, so it all ended when yet again Mrs Easton wouldn't be going home to discuss anything with Mr Easton. Because she's going out to watch drag acts at the Purple Onion in Kensington with Harry Robinson and Jock Veitch (my counterparts on the other papers) and a perfectly nice woman journalist who'll eventually join Alcoholics Anonymous.

After that Ted was a bit stumped too. Maybe a trial separation?

***

By my standards, separation had effectively begun when my father died in February 1965. North Shore Hospital called early in the morning when I was typing, and I'd looked out at the camphor laurel trees around which he'd hammered rat-and-possum-repelling tin at six o'clock on Sunday mornings, thinking he'd be happier now, in some place where one day was much like another, the way they'd been in Eumundi.

Wal didn't play tennis or dance divinely, but that could be excused by WW2 – photographs of him striding through the ruins of Hiroshima, his Air Force cap miraculously adhering to the side of his head – and I'm pretty certain that wasn't yet another thing I was just imagining, that it transformed him into the one in the slouch hat who'd strode into the mud in Flanders in WW1.

Anyway, after we'd had a row ('so when did this lunch at the Hilton finish? Where were you at three o'clock? Four o'clock?') Wal invariably sought moral and emotional support. My mother was nearly always awake, or so she claimed, and he was often there for hours, sitting on the end of her bed while the boys and I watched television.

'Look, Nick, she's going to let go of the pram! Wake up, Karl, they're about to shoot the entire royal family!'

But by 1966, shortly after I'd covered the Adelaide Arts Festival for *The Bulletin,* there'd been a night when Wal walked straight out the front door and around the corner to our English GP, Dr Peck, in Spofforth Street. Not that medical advice was going to help, but my offence this time was so heinous maybe he felt it required condemnation by a higher authority.

Like Umberto the taxi driver, Irving was another serendipitous discovery in a laundry, one of a handful of Americans hired by the New Zealand Opera Company for *Porgy and Bess.* He'd been Porgy in twenty-three countries, but in Adelaide it was only on Inia Te Wiata's nights off, so immediately we had one thing in common and soon found plenty more. Within days he'd taught me how to do double acrostic crosswords, which he'd been taught by Leonard Bernstein, and the rest of Schiller's *Ode to Joy,* provoking such pounding on the adjoining wall, around three in the morning, that we'd sing it again.

Freude, schöner Götterfunken, Tochter aus Elysium.

Wir betreten feuertrunken, Himmlische, dein Heiligtum.

Another standby was *Finian's Rainbow,* which I'd never heard of and spent years wondering who the black people were in *Finnegan's Wake.* But sometimes there was a splinter of glass which was more like a grain of sand in an oyster.

'I hear you've been sleeping with a nigger,' Dr Peck said cheerily a few days later, depressing Nick's tongue to inspect his tonsils. We'd heard whichever orchestra it was playing the Third Brandenberg? Oh, jolly good! Heard the such-and-such string quartet? Half your luck! No doubt about it, they understood music. Even their natural sense of rhythm may have been mentioned. But I know I wasn't imagining the 'I don't blame you a bit, my dear,' and the fatherly pat.

Irving had told me that his father, the pastor in Cleveland, Ohio, had lost faith in God ages ago. I'd related to that, as I was developing doubts myself about whether I wanted to become an intellectual.

Unlike Inspector Columbo on television, always shambling toward the door and then turning back, 'umm, there's just one more thing,' I'd failed to notice that women intellectuals were no longer dashing aristocrats like George Sand/Aurore

Dudevant/Merle Oberon in *A Song to Remember,*smoking cigars, wearing trousers, and having affairs with composers. [24] They were now middle class, the very thing I'd hoped to avoid. And mostly, at Rangers Road, we'd succeeded, the spirit of the Enlightenment lived on, either my mother or me showing the boys skittled dogs in gutters and estimating how long they'd been dead, buying offal instead of tinned cat food for Clea, and then for Justine, Mountolive and Sarsparilla, to demonstrate the structure and function of livers and kidneys, and sending them out in thunderstorms if I'd forgotten to buy a green vegetable for dinner. If they asked why a man was digging a hole, we'd say 'go and ask him', and always take them along if we ourselves were doing anything interesting.

So the day I went aboard a Russian whaling ship to interview the woman captain, there they were, instantly hoisted onto the shoulders of blond giants who plied them with horrible chocolate and took them below decks where they had the time of their lives, and to this day swear they never asked them if Russian sailors were still being served maggotty soup.

Like the psychotherapist and the marriage guidance woman, the new intellectuals said it never worked when young couple lived with a parent. No wonder they turned into captive housewives if they had to pay babysitters. As for servants, the very idea made them bristle with virtue.

So what if the rough occasionally outweighed the smooth, it wasn't a valid reason for junking the entire system. Thanks to Economics, I could see it was just that economies of scale were lacking, that with a larger output (if I'd had siblings) the blame per unit would have been smaller, and with a different product (if I'd been a boy), virtually negligible.

Regarding marriage, their attitude was even more extraordinary. Though I'd have given my eyeteeth for an adulterous husband, I still believed that with one you didn't want to be rid of, the sensible strategy would be to ignore it and wait for nature to take its course, as I assumed other women had done regarding me.

But the most alien concept of all was putting aged parents into a home. The only person I'd ever seen in one, during the 1951 trip to Sydney, had been my father's unmarried cousin Lexie Stewart, a WW1 nurse who possibly *had* gone to the dogs, as she'd been happily sitting up in bed reading *New Statesman,* then considered dangerously radical. [25] What really made her happy, she told us, was when the big black Commonwealth car would drive up, bearing the about-to-be knighted Governor-General William McKell, former president of the Boilermakers Union, who'd been her ward boy in Flanders.[26]

In short, Pogo was yet another American comic strip that had got it all wrong, like Al Capp had with *L'il Abner* and Daisy Mae. [27] I too had seen the enemy, and it wasn't us, because one day when the helping professionals were being more than usually obtuse, I'd rung the new Women's Electoral Lobby. 'Are you a graduate?' said a North Shore voice, not unlike that of the marriage guidance woman, in a decidedly doubtful tone.

I got the picture immediately. It was those goody-two-shoes back at St Lucia, the cashmere virgins on the sandstone steps.

Anyway it wasn't long before I was leaving home, predating the Beatles song by a few months, off to a real room of my own, a studio flat in Kirribilli, for the three months trial separation Ted thought would do the trick.

But Ted was wrong too. I was predating Andrew Lloyd Webber and Tim Rice as well, standing like Evita Peron by what would be the first of many suitcases in many halls, and never went back.

[17] Helen Gordon later lived happily with travel writer Charles Sriber until his death in June 1999.

[18] On 13 January, 1898, *L'Aurore* famously ran a letter by Emile Zola, accusing the French government of lack of evidence regarding the guilt of Captain Alfred Dreyfus, the disgraced Jewish army officer.

[19] Truman Capote, after reading Jack Kerouac's stream of consciousness novel, *On The Road,* said 'it's not writing, it's typing'.

[20] In October 2006, Sydney Imam Taj el-Din Hilaly gave a Ramadan sermon, likening women who went out, even in their own backyards, without wearing *hijab,* to uncovered meat. Cats, ie men, could not be blamed.

[21]The narrator in the English comic novel *Diary of a Nobody*, by George and Weedon Grossmith, Bradbury & Agnew, London 1892.

[22] Early eighteenth century, when English literati recalled Caesar Augustus and Virgil, Horace and Ovid.

[23] The Public Service Act was amended on 18 November, 1966.

[24] American TV series starring Peter Falk as Lieutenant Columbo, homicide detective with the Los Angeles Police Department..

[25]*New Statesman* was founded in 1913 by Sidney and Beatrice Webb with the help of George Bernard Shaw and other prominent Fabian Socialists.

[26] PM Ben Chifley wanted the Governor-General who succeeded the Duke of Gloucester to be an Australian, and is thought to have chosen a Labor man with a working class background to make a political point.

[27] Pogo, central character in Walt Kelly's comic strip about animals in the Okefenokee Swamp, Georgia.

Chapter 9
Abroad

My novel, *An Ornament of Grace*, came out a few weeks later, along with *The Permit* by Donald Horne, a former *Bulletin* editor already famous for telling Australia it was a lucky country run by second-rate people who shared its luck. Good timing, they'd be too busy being nasty about his novel to bother about savaging mine. It had a hideous cover (you think authors have any say?), I'd go into bookstores and turn copies around so people would see the photograph of me, the only decent one Wal had ever managed to take in ten years. I'm not photogenic, he says.

He'd also never shown me the photographs he'd taken ages ago, when he'd spent all day at fucking *Carlingford*, photographing some poofter who'd never amount to anything, living with some bloody Greek and breeding fucking *schnautzers*. [28] So the night my publisher takes me to Jane Street Theatre I immediately recognise the now-famous Patrick White, whom I assume meant it nicely when he said it reminded him of Edna O'Brien's. But surely this pudgy little balding man with the glasses can't be Manoly Lascaris? Where is the lithe Adonis with the wine-dark eyes, the Greek Al Pacino I've always imagined? .

***

There was another publisher, Paul Hamlyn from London, who had to be indulged because he'd just taken my Australian ones over. Upper class Pom, you know what *they're* like, they said, rustling up women for him to take to the theatre. If he asks you to dinner you'd better say yes.

It was some splendid place in Rose Bay that I'd probably already been to with Max, and seeing he'd just asked what my novel was about, I'd told him.

'You know what they're like.'

'And you were born in London?' I ask a bit later

'Berlin, acthually. Do you want to cwawl under the table now or later?'

So I'm thinking here's one who escaped before any midnight knocks on the door, and it's nice the English didn't make his father, an eminent doctor, stuff golfballs. It wasn't just Freud who'd been spared.

'I wath thwee. We were all scwubbed for dayth, lined up to gweet the gweat thage of Vienna.'

Not an adored only child, then, like Max, and probably not the apple of his father's eye even before 1943 when he became a Bevin Boy. I was still undecided about conscientious objectors, but obviously working down a coal mine was more strenuous than winding bandages, and given he's on the dainty side, some Freudian trauma is not unlikely. Anyway, I figured it explained why he still wanted to show the world how strong he'd become, the Saturday afternoon when he picked me up in Rushcutters' Park, thronged with respectable ice-cream-licking families, and threatened to dump me in a litter bin. I laughed too, not knowing that before the day is out I'll be even further surprised.

***

Although I've always found Wal's Refrigerator Guide to the Galaxy pretty reliable, with a man it's not until a woman's lying on a beach with him that she can tell what he's really like, by what he's brought to read.

Like me, Wal wasn't a beach person. But kids have to be taught to swim (*my* job, naturally, getting up at five in the morning to go to Balmoral Beach) though it was worse at weekends when he came and just sat there, with the bottom of his black gabardine trousers rolled (he only owned one pair), revealingly mortifyingly pallid ankles, reading *Playboy.* He wouldn't even buy a beach hat, and already the boys knew that a hanky knotted at the corners was the mark of the lowest type of Englishman. We'd plunge and stay there as long as possible, pretending we belonged to the cheerful bronzed fathers hurling their kids in the air, and catching them against their well-defined pecs.

But in Sydney there hadn't been time for beaches, and three months later in Acapulco Paul Hamlyn's the one who's mostly in the surf, and if he's reading anything it's something he's published, while I'm reading the new Bernard Malamud which he definitely doesn't want to know about any more than he wants to see Mayan temples. Nor does he wish to enlighten me about *dreidels* and Haman's ears. [29] Or Sukkoth and the significance of myrtle branches, leaving me to figure out about Pesach and blood libels in Czarist Russia. His friend who gave me *The Fixer* must have really hated me.

Being in the northern hemisphere I also wanted to see whether water now ran anticlockwise down the plugholes, and spent ages under the shower, which only made him worse. Hasn't he told me one inadvertent drop of Mexican water can make people direly ill for *dayths,* even *die*? Or he thinks I'm sulking about Chichen Itza, which I probably am, though it's more that I love maps – it helps to know where you are geographically, at least.

I spend a lot of time wondering at breakfast, too, why Spanish butter is called *mantequilla,* another thing it's no use asking because all he cares about is French.

'Thurely you can manage a few thententhes. Twy!'

As for keeping up appearances, with Paul Hamlyn that was

all that mattered. In New York he's pained by my colonial fur coat, my accent, the way I gaze thoughtfully out the window at the Hotel Pierre, at Central Park where I'd have loved to walk before breakfast only he says it's too dangerous. The questions I ask that he can't or won't answer, like where do the ducks go in the wintertime. [30]

'Thparkle! Look happy!'

I've no idea what he did all day, and he never asked what I'd done beyond the things which were obvious - a gorgeous silky dress, postcards from the Metropolitan Museum of Art, buttons with funny messages which evoked a feeble smile. There was a big hoarding with a munching American Indian with braids and a big black hat that I'd thought rather clever. *You Don't Have to Be Jewish to Like Levy's Rye Bread!*' He'd rather not have been Jewish at all.

And they're so smart, how come he can't tell when I *have* been sparkling? Though it's just as well, it's when I've spent all day with Irving.

That was another thing which was different in the northern hemisphere, unlike Sydney where people mostly looked at us with curiosity and even warmth, because the only black Americans had been celebrities, usually performing at the Chevron Hilton, people like Ray Charles and Eartha Kitt. True, New York wasn't exactly Alabama, and the first day, when Irving walked into the lobby of the Hotel Pierre and gave me huge hug, nothing happened, but even so ...

It was Irving who showed me the real Broadway and the chitterlings in the supermarket, who explained soul food, hush puppies, hogs' maws and grits, and drove me around Central Park, instantly laughing when I asked about the ducks. One day he drove me right up to Harlem, past children who weren't eating watermelon or romping under fire hydrants, seeing it wasn't summertime, and shabby little shops he said hadn't extended, or maybe still didn't extend, credit to black people.

I figured that was why Irving was never exactly sad about my situation, indeed quite glad after sudden business matters required Paul's attention in London and it's suggested I stay on a bit and enjoy myself.

Irving takes me home to meet his wife Gayle and teenage daughter in Queens, where there's double locks on the doors and a refrigerator twice the size of the one we had in Cremorne. His daughter reads *Ebony,* which has advertisements for creams to lighten your skin and how to straighten your hair, and tells me it's bad luck to count money while sitting on a bed. We go to a party where everyone has played in *Porgy and Bess,* or *Finian's Rainbow* somewhere, summertime or wintertime, singing until dawn when we come out to find it's been snowing all night, still drifting down like dandruff when I'd always imagined it would be more like cornflakes. But it's still the most wonderful and amazing thing, seeing it fall newborn from who knows where, when I've only seen it after it's been trodden to death on the hard grey pavements where stream blasts from the sewers in which giant alligators are said to lurk, the ones who'd no longer looked as cute as they had when you'd brought them back from Florida. .

Everyone looks at me as if I'm crazy, not understanding the bother of snow chains, until Irving explains, and soon it's even more wonderful and amazing. A Breughel landscape with black people throwing snowballs.

***

Lillian Roxon is different too in the northern hemisphere; she was always amusing but in New York she's famous rather than infamous - even Wal had been sniffy about *Weekend,* a raunchy Packer tabloid edited by Donald Horne. The word is she's unfailingly kind to any Australian new in town, so the night I'm at her place, down on the East 21st Street and perfectly safe because it's above a police station, I tell her how kind her father was to me back in Brisbane. She swore she'd never known, he always told them he'd won the money at the races.

My feeling is she's far too smart to fall for that, and she's even more miserable than I am, as Zell Rabin has just died back in Sydney, but Lillian's better than me at keeping up appearances, telling me how she's been commissioned to write an encyclopedia of rock, and about musicians she's laid, whom I assume are famous too. As if I'd know, being strictly a classics lover.

I tell Lillian about the night Wal finally got it right with the *J'accuse,* who I'd had it off with at the Adelaide Arts Festival. That it hadn't been Yevgeny Yevtushenko (or I'd have been listening to Prokofiev), or men I hadn't fancied at all, because being in an understandably buoyant mood, I'd put on one of Wal's beloved 78s, and left it on the turntable. I'm supposed to know Fats Waller was black?

It was good to be laughing with another woman, not hearing how I must have subconsciously *wanted* Wal to find out because I felt guilty and needed to suffer.

Lillian also introduced me to *I Ching*, the book of changes where you throw three coins six times and it gives an answer. She was kind about that, too

***

In England it was April, elm tree boles in tiny leaf, crocuses and squirrels in St James Park, and by July the English knew one big thing, those brave Australian gels they so admire ended up castrated at thirty in suburban redbrick bungalows. It makes me happier than I'd been for some time, as in Australia it provoked outrage for the best part of a week. Somebody even wrote 'Miss Smith said *Nova* was a frivolous magazine' but that was just them getting creative.

It was years before I got around to reading the *Nova* story again, another thing people don't always understand. That while it's No Blame, as the *I Ching* says, if your mother photographed you in the bath, aged six months, or if beehives and flares were once all the rage, with creative self-expression it's you who's responsible for any bad choices. But on the whole I think my words were well-chosen.

August I spent driving around Germany and Austria with a girlfriend from Sydney, Janet Brown, and her kids, staying in *campingplatzes* and plunging into chilly lakes. At one place, two young men from Wiener Neustadt Militärakademie, who always swam out much further, rescued our knickers off the tent rope while we'd been out during a thunderstorm. They must have seen us as exciting older women, because next thing they've put on their uniforms (and gloves) and we're being driven off for a drink, feeling faintly like we're consorting with the enemy, although WW2 ended more than twenty years ago. Over beers they tell us they like movies, but then it's *Wie sind die Marx Brothers?*

Clearly the past wasn't over, in Germany some bits hadn't even started.

***

My temporary secretarial job at *New Scientist* lasted for months once they knew I could be trusted to tidy up contributors' stories while they went to lunch in the pub. But quite often they'd take me along, and although it wasn't true about water running differently down plugholes, there was no doubt that victorious lions killed all their predecessors' progeny, wiping the slate clean so they could start creating their own, and that a lioness could spontaneously abort if she smelt the urine of a more attractive male, two things I thought feminists should be looking into. Or there'd be someone who'd just written a paper on how men's beards grew more quickly, and women's boobs swelled, when the moon was waxing.

So blame *New Scientist*, (or even men, seeing they all were) for setting me on the path to irrationality, or a little further along it, as I'd already noticed that in England people who paid attention to such things, the greater timeframe in the ecosystem above our heads, were treated with more respect. Back in Australia they'd have been asked to stare at crystal balls or read palms in a tent – at the end of a pier, as the English said.

***

In early 1968 I came back to Sydney, with three banned books stitched inside the lining of the white fur coat I never wore again, and rented a pretty little house in Paddington with Dolores from Wisconsin. She was a cocktail waitress at the Hilton who knew people on new national daily, *The Australian.*

'I hear you're pretty wild', said Walter Kommer, the chief of staff. His accent made it sound like *vile*, so I reacted with spirit and was given half the Martin Collins column. The other half was an Englishman, Arnold Earnshaw, so when people phoned in and got me, Arnold being a prodigious luncher, they'd assume I was his secretary.

Where was all this *progress* my mother had told me about? The enormous *changes* I'd notice?

Usually it was just the blindingly obvious, a thirty storey building here, some other building gone for ever, and six-lane highways. Far worse were the things conspicuous by their absence, like those lift-up seats on French buses for pregnant women and legless war veterans, and *The Guardian's* women's page. Why were supermarket cashiers still standing up and able-bodied children, upwards of two, still in strollers? In London Australians had attributed it to slushy pavements, overlooking that it happened all year round, but while the *Australian* had two other women reporters, it considered itself far too advanced to have a women's page. They were both single anyway, and one left and then the other; maybe the blokes were right, it was part of a master plan to be *Frauenfrei*.

John Douglas Pringle, the Scots-born editor of *The Sydney Morning Herald*, was a household word by now, forgiven for whatever criticisms he'd made of us in *Australian Accent*. But if he 'liberated talented women from the social page it must have been later.[31] It wasn't Fairfax policy to have women on the general staff, he said.

Actually they'd had one for ages, not in the least wild or vile. So I translated it as any woman short of menopause, and huffed off back to London. What planet were they living on?

***

In 1968 it was still possible to have stopovers without your travel agent noticing that both days would be Yom Kippur, or being told there were no right days to visit South Africa, it was a pariah state. Lordy me, if I'd been running universities, it would have been a pre-requisite for anyone intending to explore slavery – a valuable opportunity for a bit of *gnothi seauton*, knowing how easily you might succumb.

The first morning in Johannesburg began well enough with a huge fresh guava juice, another thing not yet happening in Australia, but after a day of trudging past closed shops, by nightfall I was grouchily writing postcards at the bar, where a few men seemed equally short of better things to do. So it was excellent timing after all, as the two days became three weeks.

Alan was English-born, well into his fifties, and while he didn't need to explain that architecture wasn't the most portable profession, it seemed his lovely Cape Dutch house was a foot or two short of the distance it was required to be from the dwelling of his servant Freddie, a serious offence.

· Freddie would appear at our bedside every morning with breakfast and stand by for instructions. He was a brilliant cook, but as we were mostly planning to be out the more extensive briefings were for me. Remember the Rosenbergs are Progressives. The Feldmans aren't. There were Progressive van der Merves and appallingly apartheid Wilsons, not that we met the worst sort, newly arrived Brits whose wives outraged the male servants by expecting them to wash their bras and knickers. Luckily with Nadine Gordimer you knew where you were.

She was an intense tiny woman with amazingly small feet, wearing an orange sweater and olive drab gabardine pants in a house filled with bowls of pink and purple flowers. She was then on to her fourth novel, and famous enough to have been invited to lecture at various American colleges, an experience which had left her somewhat scornful. She too had left university without getting a degree, but I think it was more that even the most liberal American academics weren't ready for writers who sent their sons to mixed-race boarding schools in Swaziland. She was also a mite scornful about her first husband, the dentist, but the interview never got around to men and we were still on books when Alan arrived. We had tea in the back garden where I heard even more about Swaziland, while thinking her garden could stand some development too, innocent of vegetables and no sign of flowers, pink, purple or otherwise.

***

At Alan's there were neat lawns, flower beds, pink syringeas and a swimming pool. I spent a lot of time lying beside it with a Campari, listening to the doves cooing differently and the intermittent burglar alarms, wondering about *Gone with the Wind* and Nazi Germany. And Freddie too had questions, which only meant more wondering.

'Did Madam come here in a boat made of reeds, like Moses?'

How did he square this religiosity, and the wife and six children back in Malawi, with his active and varied sex life, the Melnicks' nursery girl on Mondays, the Jouberts' laundry girl on Tuesdays, and so on? 'Sometimes I think it's me that's the lonely one', Alan said. I'd draw rough maps with planes crossing the Indian Ocean, but in a country with no television, for Freddie the outside world was unknown territory. What does he know of *Porgy and Bess,* or Aretha Franklin? Or care that Fats Waller was black?

Freddie's predecessor John, the one Alan said was more of a friend than a servant, and for whom he'd wangled a white-collar job, came around one day. Suit, white shirt, nice tie, he even looked a bit like Sidney Poitier, but it only made the Freddie situation worse. There wasn't just an ocean between me and Freddie, but between Freddie and John.

How amazed Freddie would have been by those huge refrigerators black people had in Queens, but then I was no less amazed by Alan's kitchen. And him an architect, like Cousin Deirdre's husband! At first I thought well, he's never had a wife, but the mortifying truth soon dawned, in South Africa wives, even mothers of six, were going out to work without the world falling apart, indeed it probably would if they didn't.

'Better a white woman than a black man', Alan explained sadly.

Irving had given me a fresh perspective on the servant question, what American blacks call 'signifying', the art of causing maximum inconvenience to your employer while having the perfect excuse. But he'd only explained it from the point of view of the signifier. I could handle Freddie's reproaches when'd catch me getting my own ice-cubes, but there was also a doomed cheese soufflé because he'd forgotten to tell me the thermostat didn't work, and a cancelled dessert.

'Madam, there is no vanilla. I will have to go by feetings to the shop.'

I imagined Freddie footsore and sweltering, forbidden to rest at *slegs vir nie blankes* bus-stops, though as I'd once walked a longish way in search of a hairdresser, I'd concluded there might not be any buses. In Inanda (think St Ives) white people wouldn't need them.

Another embarrassingly good thing about South Africa was that divorce was amazingly easy, something to do with surviving Roman-Dutch law. But there were newer, more Nuremburgish, laws, and one weekend an old friend of Alan's arrived uninvited with a crate of whisky, saying his wife was about to reveal he'd been sleeping with the nursemaid, meaning a longish stretch in prison unless Alan would swear he'd been elsewhere on the nights in question.

I know Alan declined the whisky, but if he also declined to lie, it must all have been resolved somehow because a few months later, in the South of France, he's mostly telling me about mansard roofs, or Mies van der Rohe, nothing which would spoil another memorable lunch where we'll try, not always successfully, to remember that less is more.

We also notice little punnets of cape gooseberries, and I tell him we have them in Australia too, growing in our chookyard, though in Sydney you never saw them, or the lovely jam either. The French were calling them physalis and charging around fourteen English pounds, so I predicted that in another ten years Sydney would rediscover them and we'd be paying something equally horrendous.

[28] Patrick White's *The Tree of Man*, Viking Press, NY, 1955, glowingly reviewed in the US, was deemed 'unAustralian', notably by A D Hope, poet and academic – 'this pretentious and illiterate verbal sludge.' [16/6/56].

[29] A four-sided spinning top with a Hebrew letter on each side; triangular biscuits traditionally eaten at Purim

[30] The question which obsesses Holden Caulfield in J D Salinger's *The Catcher in the Rye,* Little, Brown & Co, NY, 1951

[31] Obituary by Robert Milliken, *The Independent,* London, 11 December, 1999.

Chapter 10
Seriously Foreign

*No more falsehoods or derisions, Golden living dreams of
visions,*

Mystic crystal revelation,

And the mind's true liberation

Aquarius! Aquarius!

James Rado & Gerome Ragni, *Hair,* 1967

***

The Age of Aquarius, for me, started around October 1968,
when home became a large mansion flat in Chelsea with Maggie
the Scot, schoolteacher and lapsed RC, and Jenny the seasoned
expatriate who worked for some posh publishers in Soho and had
once gone out with an actor called Eric Idle who was about to be
famous. I was therefore soon acquainted with Tenniel, Beardsley,
Arthur Rackham, WW1 poets I'd never heard of, like Isaac
Rosenberg, and T S Eliot - so Little Gidding was an actual place,
near Cambridge, unlike Much Binding in the Marsh, or St Mary
Mead! But especially with the achievements of Jenny's glittering
friends from Sydney University, Robert Hughes, Clive James,
Richard Neville, and Richard Walsh, the editor back home at *Pol,*
the trendy new women's magazine.

One morning at breakfast we were distracted from *The
Guardian* and *New Society* by a woman in a diaphanous nightie,
striding across the rooftops in vengeful pursuit of a cat.

'It's Germs!' Jenny cried, 'Come over!' Explaining that
Germaine was living just around the corner at the Pheasantry, a
heartland of the intelligentsia, and about to become famous too.

And next thing there she was, telling us about *The Female Eunuch*. I forget what she'd changed into but a few weeks later, when we gave a dinner for six (no mean feat, in our wooden-panelled breakfast nook), she was wearing jeans, a black velvet bolero precariously joined with a safety pin, and expounding on the evils of vaginal deodorants. The two nice chaps I'd invited from *The Sunday Times* bore up splendidly, not once sliding under the table though I'm sure they'd have liked to. They liked the dinner, too, whereas Germaine's 'thanks for supper', seconds before she went out the door, struck me as taking English understatement too far. Supper wasn't a meal Australians ate, but I was pretty certain it meant something like a toasted cheese sandwich, not the three exquisite courses I'd slaved over.

***

Studio Vista, where Jenny worked in Soho, was one of several publishers who did coffee table books, art and culture for people who until recently hadn't known about either, or realised how bad English restaurant food was (or if they had, they knew it wasn't done to complain.) With eating out it helped to know French, but to avoid embarrassment with art and culture you needed to read an unwritten language, not only in paintings but in the windows and ceilings of churches, and the walls of ancient grottos and caves. That a lion, an ox, an eagle and a man is due to precession of the equinoxes, whereby every two thousand years the solstice points move back one sign, and which explained the excitement about the Age of Pisces giving way to the Age of Aquarius.

Fred Gettings, another friend of Jenny's, who lent us his car to drive around the Loire, was therefore greatly esteemed, as was Ingrid Lind who in private life was Lady somebody, the wife of a diplomat. Many were the hours I spent sitting in their sunny gardens amid the bee-loud hollyhocks, hearing about microcosms reflecting macrocosms, and speculating on whether the reverse was also true, but also discovering that for myths faced with explosion, there was also a fate-worse-than, they could merely suffer eternal simplification on the material plane. Saturn and Uranus reduced, like so much else, to good guy and bad guy.

***

Jenny was in and out of love with Ian Dunlop, a languid aristocrat who occasionally wrote waspishly for posh magazines which occasionally paid him. (I could sympathise, *Pol* too was decidedly slow). But with Maggie it was hard to tell. At least I knew it wasn't me, after she'd surprised me in the shower. Much as she loved a nice apply bottom, she said I wasn't her type, and her boyfriend Dennis didn't seem to mind, though being Canadian Chinese he could have been trying too hard to appear unflappable. He was marketing manager for Justerini and Brooks, and was often asked whether it wasn't a jolly odd career for an Eskimo.

Maggie was the first person I'd ever heard refer to the English as Sassenachs. She was also lippy with snooty shop-assistants and said withering things to flashers on trains, 'can ye no find anything better tae do wi' it?' I was dying to see a flasher so I could say it too. Actually I already had, the year before, standing at a window across the street, but I'd thought he was fondling a guinea pig.

What Maggie itched to get her hands on was That Woman! It wasn't always clear whether she meant the Queen (That Hanoverian!) or Mrs Thatcher, but after I'd interviewed her at the House of Commons I was considered heroic, though my impression was she'd been just as wary of me as I was of her. But fearing and loathing Mrs. Thatcher, even when she was only the Education Minister, was already essential for passing as an enlightened person, and listening to them despise grocers' daughters seemed a reasonable trade-off for not hearing anything derogatory about farmers' daughters, or only the posh kind.

***

Enlightened Londoners also knew everything was infinitely better in Sweden, not least their correctional facilities, one of which even allowed conjugal visits. So off I went for *The Sunday Times,* stopping off for *Pol* in Copenhagen to report on pornography, and then Småland to check out the Orrefors glass company for *Pol.* The head office was an eighteenth-century chateau, the sort where Inspector Wallender and Stieg Larsson are forever unearthing aged Nazi misogynists, but in 1969 the only other guest was an American, David Jenkins, who'd just written *Sweden: The Price of Progress.* It wasn't at all unpleasant, putting away several whiskies before dinner (as one did, the Swedes being conflicted about alcohol) and afterwards strolling by the lake, eating wild strawberries and hearing about the evils of the welfare state. Swedes had already complained to me about taxation, which they claimed was less onerous in Denmark, and boredom, though that was worse in Norway and even there the men couldn't possibly be worse than the ones in Sweden.

How they longed to be in Italy!

By now I'd decided this must be a universal phenomenon, to prevent inbreeding, but Swedish men can't have been too bad or there'd have more Swedish women in gaol for murdering their husbands. They were only in for about four years, sitting alongside the drug offenders and prostitutes who'd stolen their clients' wallets who were only there for a few months, making pretty appliquéd felt cushions on flash Husqvana sewing machines.

Definitely progress Australian women wouldn't mind paying for.

I came back to London in love with *gravad lax* and planted some dill in my window box, not realising this would soon lead to dramatic insights into the English welfare state. One morning, when as usual I was wearing my lucky tiger's eye ring - magical gemstones were all the rage - I tapped smartly on the window pane to deter a marauding pigeon, whereupon my prison story, half a ream of fresh copy paper and the carpet were covered in shattered glass, and blood dripping from my left wrist.

In Sweden, where I'd spent two days in Östersund hospital with laryngitis, my impression had been it was something Swedes were long accustomed to, foreign women being entranced by white nights and staying up too late. But in London hospitals an unmarried female colonial with a bleeding wrist and a Chelsea address, giving her name as Smith, needed constant surveillance. Not blatantly, but in a discreet English way, by someone pretending to be busy and failing dismally, which was somehow more insulting, for about three hours, until they found someone unbusy enough to insert five stitches.

Bloody idiots, Maggie said. Everyone knew you cut *along* , not across. But after Jenny moved out and Dennis frowned, saying keep an eye on Maggs, I didn't. Only bumpkins got up at daybreak, expecting everyone else to be up too. Wasn't every second woman in London reading Sylvia Plath and seeing a psychotherapist or a psychiatrist, ideally Ronald Laing who'd say it was all her family's fault? To assume she might have already tried to top herself, and might try again, would have been frightfully gauche.

That was another bad morning, working out how many Mogadons Maggie had taken and hauling her back and forth until the ambulance men arrived. But within months it was worse, I'd become an undesirable alien, along with thousands of other Commonwealth citizens unable to enjoy Europe for fear the

English wouldn't let us back in, which Australians saw as typical English hypocrisy, not to admit their real worry was black ones. But to me hypocrisy meant feigning a non-existent virtue, like the diligence aspired to by the person preventing me from further self-harm at St George's Hospital, whereas a blanket prohibition looked more like sloth, taking the easy way out instead of spending a few hard days' nights figuring where to draw the line. And guilt, too, when England was already overcrowded, to still be letting in the Irish, averse to contraception and frequently unemployed.

Whatever it was, I resolved to become one of the unintended consequences. With documentary proof of one Irish-born grandparent you could get an Irish passport, so I wrote several letters to Wexford parish priests, always enclosing ten pounds for the orphans' fund, even invented legitimate excuses to go to Ireland but all I learnt was *slainte* and how to pronounce Siobhan.

Victor Bizannes, a lawyer and another of Jenny's university friends, was having no luck either pursuing one of my girlfriends, but he'd found a mentor, a charming Viennese lawyer called Hans Marcus.[32] So soon I'm in Dublin again, where an Irish lawyer says I can stop enriching Wexford postmen, all the parish records had been removed to Dublin early in the century and are lost forever.

For a moment I'm thinking rotten Papist bastards, dear old Mina's right. But the enemy's enemy is my friend and for fifteen guineas he's happy to get me listed in the *Clar na mBreitheanna Coigriche*, or Foreign Births Register, free forever more to say what I like about the Irish, and the legitimate holder of a bottle green passport with a gold harp, who has *dath na sul* (green eyes) and *dath na gruaige* (red-brown hair).

So *slainte* to Michael Collins, or whoever blew up the Public

Records Office in 1922.

***

Maggie was in the Maudsley Hospital for months, so it got rather lonely in the Chelsea flat, but Hans Marcus fixed that too, and maybe I should also thank whoever had recently burgled the rooftop apartment, in Holland Park, of his old friend David Weizman, QC, who was out all day and far into the night at the House of Commons, and didn't want it happening again.

Naturally they hadn't made off with the sculptures, which had belonged to David's late second wife, the sister of Hephzibah Menuhin's second husband, Richard Hauser, an Austrian sociologist and doer of good works in the East End. [33] All this I'd hear on Saturday mornings when we'd sit on the terrace, David contentedly puffing his pipe and setting aside his responsibilities as MP for Hackney to fill me in on his father who'd emigrated from Poland, and the famous Chaim, whom I think was an uncle.

I'd only been in Israel for three days and as Denis O'Brien, one of our more perceptive English migrants, had recently pointed out in *Pol,* Australians judged people's opinions by how long they'd spent in a place, the most recent offender being Arthur Koestler, (a few weeks, in November, 1968.) [34] So nobody got to read about old men eating black forest cake in midsummer in Dizengoff Street - shades of my grandfather/Uncle Wilfred in his spats - and the melting snow which dripped steadily down my neck from the furry brim of the yeshivah student's hat on the bus back from Jerusalem. They want me telling them, back in Sydney, that White Christmas cards aren't as ridiculous as they think?

The part-time housekeeper, Mrs Cole, knew nothing of Israel, and if she'd heard of the class struggle it made no difference, she'd voted Tory all her life, same as her husband, which never failed to horrify the London Australians. So I didn't mention either that I thought it rather sweet, the way she'd run after

David in the mornings, like Nanny Hawkins pursuing the young Sebastian Flyte

'Sir Dear, you've forgotten your umbrella! Sir Dear, remember your bad chest and wrap up well!'

***

That year the media were excited about a different struggle. The Palestinians, including the beautiful Leila Khaled, were hijacking planes, so I really should have predicted a further paradigm shift in my identity, one of those knocks on the door at ten minutes to midnight. My first thought was he's exactly like every English copper in the movies, all reassuring and deferential, but after that all I'm noticing is the *mezuzah* on the door.

'Nothing to be alarmed about, Mrs Weizman, but perhaps it would be wise for month or so? Any suspicious-looking persons?'

I drank quite a bit of David's Scotch while I waited for him to come home, trying to figure how you'd be able to tell – if someone's planning to kill you, surely they'd go to some lengths *not* to look suspicious? But David was right, they'd got it all wrong and they didn't kill his cousin either, Chaim the chemist in Golders Green.

Shortly afterwards there was a by-election, so I helped out in Hackney where it was me who got it all wrong, stricken that so many Jewish people (the sort Max would have crossed the street to avoid) were spurning my proffered leaflets. But back at the office everyone thought it hugely funny – in Stamford Hill, elections or no elections, Saturday is the Sabbath – and offered me a chopped liver sandwich, meaning well, I suppose, though I'd have preferred a *latke*. Another curious thing to think about, that in Eumundi we'd eaten them for breakfast at least once a week, never realising it was ethnic cuisine. But it seems I'm wrong there, too, real *latkes* need a drop of blood in them, from your scraped knuckles after grating the potatoes, to show you've suffered.

***

All those writers and composers whose hearts leapt up when they beheld Italy! Bursting forth like chaffinches because the sun shines for days or even weeks on end. Today they'd be on medication for seasonal affective disorder, but in 1970, as my train approached Verona, everyone already perilously leaning out the windows, I was more than ever persuaded that the point of departure, ie arrival, in time and space, was what mattered. What if Tchaikovsky, let alone Dostoyevsky or Sibelius, had been born in Italy, or Rossini in Sweden or Russia? And even then there were exceptions, Robert Browning hankering to be in England in April, when for T S Eliot April is the worst month?

But there was Grazia on the platform, and for the next six weeks the only Italian I learnt was at the hairdressers (*il principe Carlo* was definitely gay) because I'm there to stop her and Sergio forgetting the English they'd learnt in London.

Sergio was of noblish birth, an executive at the Glaxo factory which already had an on-site crèche, and Grazia taught primary school, so after lunch and a small siesta she'd walk me around Romeo-and-Juliet-related places, and sneer at antique repro furniture in store windows while she lit yet another cigarette. I hadn't thought Italian women would smoke in the street.

'My problem is I have no problems,' she tells me.

In Sweden, women had been worrying about unhappy far-off people, those Kurds I could never find in the atlas, and in England it was Czech dissidents or African dictators. But in Rome, at her mother's, Grazia brightened noticeably. One of her brothers was a film director – spaghetti westerns were big – and when they came home for lunch they'd often bring their wives and become tremendously excited, heaven knows what about but

120

if I'd heard the word Mussolini I'd have made an effort, being curious to know what else they might think he was wonderful for, apart from draining the Pontine marshes and fixing malaria.

Grazia's mother was another early riser, so I'd often join her in the kitchen because she spoke a bit of French.

'*Pour le chien?*' She's fixing something sloppy with gravy, and there's a dog.

'*Espèce de chien,*' she says darkly, pointing upstairs.

I'd no idea there was a grandfather on the premises, but it was nice they were still feeding him, even if they didn't need him, when he was sixty-four or whatever and losing his teeth, and hadn't persuaded him to see himself as a *burden*. Like the on-site crèches, it seemed further evidence of a cyclic universe, that Italy was so un-progressive it was actually ahead of its time.

***

As a photographer's wife, one thing I must have noticed in the 1960s was Bob Guccione starting the more explicit *Penthouse* to compete with Hugh Hefner's *Playboy*. But that's the trouble with shifting downmarket, your readers don't faff around with psychotherapists. They want advice, smartish, about problems which are all too visible, penises which are too small, too thin or a funny colour, and sometimes, if not always, performing less than heroically. So for the sake of male honour a second magazine was created, *Forum: the International Journal of Human Relations,* entirely devoted to medical, psychological and sometimes legal reassurance and written by women, mostly in a strictly-from-hunger situation like myself – Faye from Brooklyn, Anna Raeburn the resting actress and Maddy the single mother.[35]

But it couldn't have been just me who'd never heard about the American quiz show scandal back in the Fifties.[36] All anyone knew was that Al Freedman, the editor, could never work in the

States again. He was always pretty twitchy, so if all four of us confronted him, ('sisterhood is powerful!' said Faye) we'd usually win and there'd be yet another story about every woman being different, not one big homogenous blob as Freud seemed to think, asking what do women want? When the only thing all women had in common was being oppressed by patriarchs.

I'd thought only Orthodox Greeks had patriarchs, but as Faye soon made clear, in America patriarchs meant the medical profession and Madison Avenue.

Nobody at *Forum* ever went to the pub, not even Gabriel, the only male writer. He looked like a young Marcel Proust and being an Oxford man got to write the classier stories, *Sodomy in the Royal Navy*, and *Schubert's Tragic Secret*, keeping his head down even when Faye wasn't asking us how to spell phimosis, or balanitis, or explaining how Aborigines performed total sub-incision of the penis. But mostly she'd be on about the iniquities of Freud, Adorno's authoritarian personalities, the goodness of Fritz Perls, Kurt Lewin and Abraham Maslow and the badness of Bruno Bettelheim, for seeing meaning in outmoded sexist fairy tales and saying refrigerator mothers caused autism.

To raise the awareness of English readers regarding the Age of Aquarius, we re-wrote American letters from back issues, relocating sadomasochists to Grimsby and Reading, and populating staid regional cities with leather fetishists. The trickier letters were sent to experts, including those about postnatal sexual difficulties, and here Faye was horribly right, endless horror stories of epidurals, caesareans, episiotomies, and being sewn up too tight.

By summer, after a gourmet tour of Hungary, I could report that Budapest had a statue of Ignaz Semmelweis, martyred for attributing puerperal fever to doctors' failure to wash their hands after dissecting corpses. [37] But regarding the Orthodox women in

New York who were restoring a rundown *mikveh*, arguing that the monthly purification bath for women was a deeply meaningful tradition, I kept shtum. It sounded too close to Isaac Bashevis Singer, whom I suspected was held in even lower regard than Bruno Bettelheim.

Towards the end of the year, there was a phone call from Rangers Road, not from my mother but from Wal's wife, about his job that was on the line at *Woman's Day* and maybe it would be good if I came back.

For women who'd once seemed so smart, they'd taken an awful long time about it.

***

[32] Hans Marcus, a German-Jewish émigré lawyer, specialised in retrieving Holocaust survivors' money and property.

[33] In 1955, after divorcing Australian grazier Lindsay Nicholas, Hepzibah Menuhin married Richard Hauser, Austrian Quaker sociologist, social commentator and father of Sydney feminist Eva Cox. Returning to London, they founded the Institute for Human Rights and Responsibilities, the Centre for Group Studies, and a settlement house in the East End.

[34] Koestler, invited by Barry Jones to speak on his TV show, *Encounter,* was reportedly so 'petulant and arrogant' that many of the audience walked out.

[35] Anna Raeburn became a famous agony aunt.

[36] *Quiz Show*, 1994. The producers arranged for Herb Stempel/John Turturro to lose out to the more fashionable Charles van Doren/Ralph Fiennes, a social studies lecturer at Columbia.

[37] In 1865 Ignaz Semmelweis, clinically depressed, was sent to a Viennese insane asylum. Straitjacketed in a darkened cell, regularly doused with cold water and dosed with castor oil, he died two weeks later.

Chapter 11
1973-75 - Ex-expatriate Blues

The *Forum Australia* office in Woollahra was in a handsome historic building on the corner of Queen and Moncur, a short step from the Packer mansion but a giant leap from the former pie factory in South Kensington. The launch party, spilling into the palmy courtyard of the flower shop next door, was orchestrated by Spasm, the agency run by Clyde's mate John Singleton, who'd had no trouble finding guests who'd lend verisimilitude and gravitas to an otherwise blatantly raunchy enterprise. Among them was Tina Arndt's father, Professor Heinz Arndt the economist, with whom I attempted polite conversation about Ludwig von Mises and Friedrich Hayek. He still looked as if he'd rather be elsewhere.

Up to a point, I shared his pain. It wasn't just the media, as it was now called, exulting that Australia, as well as producing a world-class iconoclast, now had its very own authority on varieties of clitoral experience. And the tyranny of distance, the traditional excuse for just about everything, was no longer just geographical, it had become historical, as if until *The Female Eunuch* no Australian woman had ever said boo to a goose. So Tina and I had been immediately labelled women's libbers, though neither of us were hairy-legged lesbians.

Once, too, people had joked about how there was nothing wrong with Australia that couldn't be fixed by towing it away and anchoring it off the coast of Europe, forgetting there'd already been a metaphorical relocation in the opposite direction. I'd forgotten myself, after four years with nary a priest or a nun to be seen, and pitying all those poor Irish women on the ferry looking queasy on the way over and guilty on the way back. In England, abortion and contraception had been yesterday's problems. I'm pretty certain most Englishwomen hadn't needed permission to masturbate, either. But what could you say that wouldn't end in someone telling you to go back where you came from, if it was so good?

At *Forum UK,* childrearing never got further than toilet-training, a crucial determiner of sexual performance, but an Israeli study had found that kibbutz children rarely, if ever, showed sexual interest in people they'd sat next to at potty time. Until then, incest had been attributed to overcrowding; poor families living in tenements and tarpaper shacks, and the study paved the way for Herbert Maisch, who said the more usual perpetrators were either fathers returning from lengthy absences, or incoming stepfathers. It didn't sound too far from *New Scientist,* the incoming lions killing their predecessor's progeny, so I wrote a review, pointing out that a girl's, or a boy's, worst enemy might be mum's boyfriend. Tina said much the same, only for different reasons.

But by 1973, Australian women couldn't have too many boyfriends, or too few children. Maybe that explained why they weren't noticing those able-bodied tots in strollers were steadily getting bigger, and more often consuming something unwholesome. What had happened to *spoilt*? But again, what could I say, and it wasn't just the expatriate thing. After five years of sitting in those sunny gardens, mastering sidereal time and degrees of right ascension (my maths improved dramatically) I'd been turned as surely as Burgess, Maclean and Philby, so when Tom Wolfe came up with 'the Me Generation', our people, who also knew a thing or two about lions, saw it as further confirmation of the wondrous workings of the universe. Whatever the cause, the ingress of Pluto into Leo in 1940 had definitely been a marker.

But for those on the Right the cause was plain to see – Dr Benjamin Spock's *Baby and Child Care,* which had produced a generation of pampered brats refusing to go and fight Commies. Admittedly the night I'd met him he'd been speaking at an anti-war rally alongside Vanessa Redgrave, and while I'd been in two minds about Vietnam, I saw no reason not to tell him I loved his book.

If the Australian Right had reached this conclusion unaided, rather than via Norman Vincent Peale the American televangelist, it would have been bad enough, but either way it showed neither knew about Dr Spock's predecessors, Dr Truby King who believed in minimal mother-baby contact, and the loathsome behaviourist John Broadus Watson who persuaded mothers that cuddling their little boys would turn them into homosexuals. Scarcely evidence of intellectual rigour. It was like saying guns were bad because they killed people, which was what the Left said.

That was probably why I'd tried to chat up Tina's father, hoping as a foreigner he'd say something intelligent, as by English standards there wasn't a Right in Australia, just men who'd stopped being Left.

Also, when I'd been growing up I'd thought it was just our family, but by 1973 Australia was full of people who'd stopped being something quite recently, and one thing I knew, apostasy wasn't something you recovered from overnight. If Mina and Ollie were any indication, even a hundred years mightn't be long enough. Why else were they all reading *A Hundred Years of Solitude,* about levitating priests in Latin America, and babies born with pigs' tails?

Besides, until now every apostate I'd known had opted for the methadone approach, just moving down a notch or two. They hadn't done it cold turkey and become atheists, which according to popular wisdom had been the other fast track to becoming a Commie, for those who didn't go to university.

Here I was short on primary evidence apart from Phillip Adams, the day I'd set out thinking it'd be another rich-and-famous-despite-leaving-school-at-fifteen story, and wound up hearing all about the wicked stepfather and the puppy-drowning. But Phillip had stopped being a Communist in 1956, when most people did, and by now I'd concluded that anyone in Sydney who'd ever strung more than two sentences together had joined the Eureka Youth League. It was a rite of passage, like sharing a taxi with Bea Miles.

Still, Phillip didn't seem the sort who'd shoot farmers, or their livestock or daughters, and neither did Alex Mitchell, a Queenslander and committed Trotskyite who'd been instrumental in getting me hired by *The Sunday Times*. Besides, they were men and unlike the Chekov play where there's only three sisters yearning to go to Moscow, in Sydney there were hundreds who already had, metaphorically, and saw me as a pioneering feminist because I'd left my husband and children. A mere nothing, like Jane Fonda makes it seem in *The Doll's House*.

But I was back in a country which didn't do metaphors, or markers either, or not beyond the moon's phases correlating with tides. And why would anyone bother catching fish, or women learn to cook them, now you could buy frozen ones?

***

Patriarchs were now as common as rabbits had been, pre-myxomatosis, and according to dear old Mina, my own grandfather had been one of them.

'If Uncle Wilfred gave a pig to those Chinese gardeners down by the creek for their New Year, it was just so they'd keep giving him a dozen silk handkerchiefs and jars of pickled ginger at

Christmas. Poor Annie's name never to be mentioned again, and expecting his younger sisters to wait on him hand and foot. Lucky for them those Spry boys turned up.'

I remembered Uncle Courtney Spry who'd talked to bees, though not Uncle Arthur, the bank clerk in Sydney who'd talked to pot plants and whose children were now millionaires. They were said to have a nephew who worked in Canberra, whom we'd assumed could be safely forgotten. [38]

The Packers had been patriarchal for two generations but Clyde, unlike the teetotal Kerry, was overweight and given to fleshly pleasures, like long lunches in Darcy's or Madame de Farge's where he'd unburden himself to Tina and me about his sufferings at the hands of Sir Frank. Clyde lived in Queen Street, and some Saturday mornings he'd amble down to the *Forum* office in a brown and white floral toga and flip-flops, looking like a tropical Tiberius. The last person I'd seen at large in a state of *deshabille* had been in Paddington, an old bloke popping out to the corner shop for milk and cigs in a dressing gown like the one Wal's mother bought him at Gowings. In Cremorne a man had roamed the streets in his underwear, but he'd escaped from a private hospital, so I figured it was only done by the working class and the aristocracy, which by Australian standards the Packers were.

In London I'd defied Australia by sending the boys *Private Eye*, which ran the Barry Mackenzie strip, and as Clyde was now helping Barry Humphries quit drinking, and had just given me a pre-loved black glass coffee table, I was able to give a lunch at my place.[39] Barry barely spoke, moodily drawing on a paper napkin while Tina and I indulged Clyde with stories about Xaviera (*The Happy Hooker*) Hollander, and later showed us a desperate man gripping prison bars shaped like penises.

It reminded me of Wal's narrative, how one Sunday he and

his mother convinced his father they were going on picnic, knowing there'd be men waiting, who'd clanged the iron gates shut. He and his mother walking briskly down the gravel drive, hearing him curse them to beyond the grave.

Another day Tina and I took Germaine to Eliza's in Double Bay, where Clyde had promised to join us later, to hear about the evils of hormone replacement therapy. As with the vaginal deodorants, I entirely agreed, only it took a bottle of Dom Perignon before we'd even looked at the menu, and then another after she'd spilt a glass on what looked like a nice but quite ordinary black dress.

'Oh Jesus, my Jean Muir!'

Every head swivelled, but as I'd just got my first credit card I was more worried about how much abuse that could stand, should Clyde fail to show. But I certainly wasn't *cringing* – a word they're still perversely attached to, a sort of cultural discomfort blanket seventy years after abruptly weaning themselves from Britain. Cringing, as every dog-owner knows, is a vertical action, abasement before something superior, and closer to grovel, whereas wincing is more horizontal, to create distance from undesirable behaviour in someone of whom you'd expected better, as with cats whose owners put them in red antlers at Christmas.

But already you could predict they'd need help with body language, the way they thought the Muscovines terribly clever for asking men 'what part of 'no' don't you understand? Obviously they'd never owned a horse. Even when I wrote a story for *Cleo,* about how horses taught little girls to handle inarticulate creatures larger than themselves, it got called *Great Galloping Orgasms.*

Irony too was wasted. In *Bring Back Chaperones*, I argued it would make dating less stressful and restore the excitement of delayed gratification – men might even start reading poetry to us, though by now I was wincing at poetry too. As if Freud hadn't already set them off how *'they fuck you up, your mum and dad'* we needed Philip Larkin reminding them?

The Adyar bookshop, the traditional refuge for our people, still smelt of India, but now it was awash with books on what they were calling the New Age, as if India were another amazing new discovery. It was better upstairs where the Jung Society met, hearing psychiatrists stressing the importance of male initiation rites (otherwise men went to the dogs and women wound up doing all the work) and the propensity of some women to fall in love with men doing ten years for armed robbery, at which we'd nod sagely about Neptune in the seventh house. But it was bricks and mortar houses that were occupying my mind now Victor Bizannes was back in Sydney and married to my girlfriend. He'd helped make me an Irish citizen, maybe he could make me a woman of property.

It was my first time in a courtroom so I was remembering Aunt Linda, the first crucified Smith woman, and even Cousin Deirdre, who couldn't have been more than eight when she'd found her father hanging in the barn. Years later she told me she remembered her plaits dangling over the edge of the dock and one ribbon coming undone. She was driving me somewhere at the time, as people often are when they tell you appalling things.

Victor established that my mother had paid the deposit and, despite the absence of receipts, that I'd contributed to the household expenses. So Wal's barrister played the man, which I'd now learnt was Australian for *ad hominem*.

Was I not considerably *younger* than my husband? An attractive woman who'd have no trouble getting a job as a receptionist? He'd have added 'or another husband,' if I hadn't smartly protested, whereupon the judge intervened, maybe thinking this attractive and thrifty little earner deserved a break, and ruled that I needn't wait for Nick to finish university, I'd get my half-share of the house when he finished high school.

***

Surprisingly, Wal made no fuss about taking Nick to Bali for Christmas 1975, not like when *I'd* had to get a passport, dark hints and midnight phone calls about his good friend in the Immigration Department who'd stop me in my tracks. But for Nick tiny topless brown women selling fruit on the beach weren't enough, he itched to go up to Kuta Beach and see big topless white ones. So we did, hiring bikes and taking in a Hindu tooth-filing, an initiation rite he watched without a tremor. But the morning we got up at three to catch a bus for a ferry for the slow train to Jogjakarta (Borobudur, in the chocolate atlas!) he complained of colicky pains, so off I went and worried for the next three days. *Teenager's Lonely Death, Mother Abandons Dying Son to Seek God,* when he'd only been smoking Kreteks with sundry Mrs. Robinsons and telling them he's at university. Is it my fault I'm unacquainted with teenage males' infinite capacity for cunning plans?

But regarding sexual aspirations, those rupiahs I put on the elephant shrine could well have done the trick.

***

Despite the Muscovines, I still believed it was women's nature to make allowances for foreigners. So although I'd been initially gob-smacked when Steve told me the world was getting better, I figured it was something he'd picked up when he used to take his mother to St Spyridon's on Sunday, and then sit outside on the steps smoking and discussing Marx and Nietzsche with the Greek equivalent of the ice-maidens at St Lucia, which I'd now concluded must be a universal urban phenomenon. If it wasn't university, it'd be places like Gould's Third World bookstore. [40]

Saturdays his family would go to Balmoral or Manly on the tram, coming home with buckets of pippies on their knees and getting dirty looks. Australians didn't know what they were missing, he'd tell me. His parents' point of arrival had been Surry Hills, shortly before Ruth Park was living there writing *The Harp in the South*, and his mother still believed all Australian women fed their children on fish and chips, or left them to open a tin of baked beans while they went to the pub. He had a name with even more potential for innocent merriment than mine, and for a while he'd called himself Patterson.

I don't *look* Greek, do I? he'd ask, in his sweet serious way.

It would have been cruel to say yes, that it was probably a major reason, along with too much ouzo and Theodorakis.

***

Early in the next century, the night his wife phones to say Steve has died, it was like the night I'd met Manoly Lascaris, a week after I'd left Wal, because now I'm the only person who could have told her what Steve once looked like. The Sunday morning when he's standing in front of the mirror, in a crisp white shirt and having a little trouble with his gold cufflinks, when I can see myself in the mirror too, lying in bed and wishing he didn't have to go to the stone setting or that I could go too to see what Greeks did. Not that there isn't a certain pleasure in looking at dark hairy wrists emerging from pristine white cuffs, civilisation mocked by ineradicable evidence of a sweaty animal past. Though on another level, I'm wondering if it isn't God moving in a mysterious way, to make women appreciate what a miracle it is that men have come so far, dutifully attending stone settings, saying *kaddishes* and observing holy days, when they could be staying sweaty and animal in bed with me.

It doesn't occur to me Freud might be right, that what I'm seeing is my father setting off alone for Kenilworth, driven by more secular obligations. Back then I'm thinking more of van Eyck, (so well remembered from my uncles' art books), Jan Arnolfini and his wife coyly bulging in her green velvet dress, reflected in a more distant convex mirror.

As they'll put it later, it seemed like a good idea at the time.

***

The Mike Walsh Show, the first Australian live-to-air chat show, also had only one male writer, as women were considered better at persuading reluctant people. There weren't many, most being only too keen to tell how they were fighting some force of darkness (governments, councils, but never Catholicism – Mike adored nuns) or had been raped, or had a vasectomy. Sometime we'd weaken and pay twenty-five dollars to those who made enough fuss, usually people in the newer professions, but it was considered pushy.

Public relations ensured that most celebrities, local and international, stayed to join one or two of the scriptwriters for a panel discussion of some contentious issue like mixed flats, tattoos, or piercing babies' ears. But occasionally one failed to show and we'd have to think of a disease, phone Dr James Wright down the road in Epping and then rustle up somebody who'd admit to having it.[41] With morning sickness I'd have volunteered myself, pretending I'd had it, but I'd been on camera already that week, having my own ears pierced. Luckily someone knew a Jeannie Little, so after a long chat on the phone (she'd never heard of raspberry leaf tea!), she turned up in a white dress with pink elephants appliquéd around the hem, and never looked back.

Coming out of the closet wasn't easy, admitting I hadn't just been waiting until the time was right (what was medical science for, if not to beat biological clocks?). I tried telling them that at forty it takes more than just looking at a pair of trousers, indeed

I'd been wondering if I shouldn't give up on the revolting herbal concoctions and go crawling back to Dr Jules Black, a friend of Tina's and a *Forum* adviser who'd become my gynaecologist.

'And where are we having this baby?'

I'd explained it was not a question of *we*, not easy when you're flat on your back and the rejected party, whom you have nothing against personally, is removing your IUD. As bad as having to drown puppies.

***

Hopewood Health Farm had been one of my more distant assignments with Wal, a heartland of fasting, enemas and nettle soup. So in 1975, when only Nimbin hippies had home births, it was the logical place to look for a midwife.

Another thing which had just been scientifically proven, falling into the somewhat rarer category of things most people had known all along, was burn-out, that once some occasional and enjoyable task turned into a nine-to-five profession, you became sloppy or callous. And as Edith Gosling said, birthing babies, along with laying out the dead which midwives had also once done, was another thing best interwoven with traditional women's work. But for the Muscovines the new big thing for women was 'non-traditional' careers, meaning everything men used to do and still did.

I gave parties on my balcony, and spent happy hours making *spanakopita* and *taramasalata* (you could still buy real cod's roe then) and sticky orange and almond cake. Not that there weren't some unexpected events. But afterwards it seemed rather touching, all those women not wanting it on their conscience if I'd died in childbirth and they hadn't returned my *Zen and the Art of Motorcycle Maintenance*, or *The Tibetan Book of the Dead*.

It all went splendidly, and afterwards we sat on the bed drinking champagne and eating strawberries, watching the sun come up behind the poplars at the edge of what was then the ABC car park. It was a Monday public holiday but within hours. The Walsh Show had sent enough flowers for a Mafia funeral, then Tina arrived with more (and Dennis Minogue carrying a six-pack), and by lunchtime, Jules Black with his two little girls. He didn't whip back the sheets seeking evidence of negligence, or a dried newt or frog's tongue, but a small shameful part of me hoped he would, because there weren't any.

***

[38] Brigadier Sir Charles Chambers Fowell Spry, CBE, DSO, headed ASIO from 1950 to 1970.

[39] *The Wonderful World of Barry McKenzie,* based on the *Private Eye* comic strip by Nicholas Garland, was banned in Australia, the Department of Customs and Excise declaring it indecent.

[40] In 1969 Bob Gould, a notable activist, was found guilty of publishing obscene articles - Aubrey Beardsley posters of Lysistrata and Cinesius Pursuing Myrhenia.

[41] Dr James Knight, a prominent Seventh Day Adventist –doctors who became media personalities had to use a pseudonym to avoid being deregistered.

Chapter 12
Motherhood Revisited

In the 1970s Australians weren't yet required to pamper foreign students with home stays - hot meals, en suites and family ambience, as in a husband, kids and a Labrador. Anyone with a spare room could put up a notice in the nearest English language college, though I never heard of anyone who did except my old friend Jenny, who now lived in Brisbane and wrote glowingly about a Mayumi who taught her to make origami cranes and chicken teriyaki. Lodgers, as we'd called them in London, must have been another part of the shameful British heritage of which Southerners had disencumbered themselves.

That was another tribulation our people had to endure, everyone assuming we must be psychic, but it hardly took clairvoyance to see Japanese boys would be perfect - reliable payers who'd never get drunk, couldn't cook (so they'd never be underfoot in the kitchen) and by nightfall dutifully studying or out with other Japanese. And *New Scientist* was right, they *did* shave less often and spent less time in the bathroom too. A few arrived with a rice cooker, for which their mothers sent special rice wrapped in manga comics, so that's probably true too, that they keep young men out of trouble.

The only challenge, as they now say, was years later when the kid and I were watching *A Town Like Alice*, Bryan Brown being crucified to a door just as Takeshi and his mates came home. But it's those first seven years that count. *They're more afraid of you than you are of them.*

They stand there transfixed for several minutes and eventually say 'Japanese Army very bad. Not Japanese people'.

Quite.

***

A few times I spoke on home birth to the Family and General Practitioners' Society, how when I'd gone into labour Edith had said 'aha, you're watching *Summer of '42'*. They chuckled and said that's what they'd been taught in the 1940s, after the seventh month pregnant women should avoid emotional situations, as in weddings, funerals and listening to Bing Crosby. Luckily the President was Dr Eric Fisher, as by 1975 the next near-impossible thing to find in Sydney after a homebirth midwife was a doctor who'd still do circumcisions. (Whatever had become of balanitis and phimosis?)

Naturally I'd been too busy to notice the Whitlam dismissal, but Steve's friends soon pointed that thanks to him, tertiary education was now free. Abusing the system? It was a positive duty to acquaint my ethnic child with his rich cultural heritage.

Modern Greek 1, externally at the University of New England, was another Anglo-Sax situation, or possibly Anglo-Celtic – me, a couple of nuns, and a pharmacist from Wollongong who wanted to communicate better with his customers. But we didn't discover this until the first residential week in May, or that once past 'I'll be home late, Mum, keep my dinner warm', most of the Greeks knew no more than we did.

That too shouldn't have been hard to foresee. With my homework assignments it had never been the aorist, aka preterite, tense, as in Steve having a headache once. It was definitely imperfect, he had them continually. Or problems with his glasses. Luckily our lecturer was an Australian woman who'd fallen in love with Greece (which I translated as a man who'd looked like Steve, or Manoly Lascaris pre-WW2), so she'd answer all our questions before we'd even asked them, and the chemist and the nuns too could have finished the year with a Distinction.

Steve had wooed me with Cavafy's *Body Remember*, the voyage to Ithaka which would bring the lovely discoveries and the Laestrygonians who could not harm me.[42] But the more susceptible of our people, persuaded that mothers played no role in one's success in the real world, and that nurture could only translate as babies, now believed that spending your birthday in another city might ensure a better year, whereas my money was on Cavafy, wherever you moved to the same four walls would follow you around and you'd screw up the same old way according to your natural propensity. Which was why, on 14 February 2008, I went slogging through muddy Alexandrian streets, clutching a scentless red rose thrust upon me by a waiter at the Hotel Cecil and passing yet more red teddy bears and heart-shaped balloons, to find the actual room on the Rue Lepsius, now Sharia Sharm el-Sheikh, wherein Cavafy grasped this metaphysical truth. Only to find it's just me, and the visitors' book is all tour groups from Greece, with only a rare Chris and Nick from San Francisco or Denver.

But as 1976 wore on Cavafy was being eclipsed by Chile, and the last thing a woman needs is a man telling her about military dictatorships when she's bathing a slippery baby after a hard day's typing (in this regard, Steve was no better). And as well as inventing stories for *Pol* and *Cleo,* I'd had to create a terse letter to UNE, who'd written after the residential week that Father O'Whatsis had been most irate. St Albert's men's college sullied by a woman with a baby!

Far more serious were the irreconcilable differences which now emerged about everything else. It was cruel, the way Anglo Saxons put babies to bed so early!

'Well, of course,' I'd tell him. 'Bath them around sunset, put your feet up, start breastfeeding, with luck they're asleep before you've finished your first gin and tonic. No wonder Greek women look sixty by the time they're thirty.'

But Steve wasn't buying it, which was what it mostly came down to – buying, and being seen to have bought, especially clothes. Even if my family *had* been churchgoers, humungous weddings and funerals would still have been a foreign concept. Until he was seventeen or so, a boy had no need of long trousers, let alone patent leather shoes and dinner jackets.

'Life's so hard when you get older,' Steve would tell me. 'That's why you have to indulge children when they're young.'

'That's *why* it's so hard,' I'd say.

***

Jean Liedloff's *The Continuum Concept* was all the rage and the kid spent his first year sleeping with us in the Art Nouveau bed I'd found in the second-hand shop in Crown Street. So every so often I'd invent another terse letter, asking why babies in Amazon jungles, and Africa, were never inadvertently smothered by sleeping parents.

According to *Forum UK,* it was what mothers of one-too-many said in confession, confident that priests weren't in a position to argue. But I never heard that in Australia, or that co-sleeping and breastfeeding would solve the serious feminist issue of who got up to fix bottles, and though they now approved of fathers being present at the birth, I'd gone back to thinking it was women's business. Besides, I could remember women in the Thirties saying wouldn't it be lovely, men would soon change once they saw all the agony they caused.

But either I hadn't suffered enough or in some men, Jung's *pueri aeterni,* fatherhood never switches on, the ability to foresee impending disasters and pay attention to the here and now. Perhaps that's why I gave up on *A Hundred Years of Solitude,* Colonel Aurelio Buendia facing the firing squad and all he can think about is the distant afternoon when his father took him to see the miracle of ice.

A few years later I was writing a *Pol* story about Peter Clyne, maverick tax accountant and authority on the late Hapsburg empire, who was living in the Sebel Town House post-divorce. He said it had happened after he'd asked his wife Densey, a noted conservationist, to choose between him and her spiders, which was pretty much what Steve had done regarding the cat sleeping with us too. Yet another thing Anglo-Saxon women did wrong, like shaving their armpits, which he said only prostitutes did.

The Muscovines were right, though, it was time to think about my own needs, and what could any woman need, especially one who'd seen off Father O'Whatsis, but a degree in Gender Studies or Marxism? Or French, to shine at dinner parties? (David Williamson was terribly in.)

But if biology was destiny, shouldn't 'know thyself' involve how the human body actually worked, apart from the bits below the waist? (Another freelancer, Annabel Frost, swore *Cleo* once asked her for a picture of a hormone.) Besides, as an Old Believer I could now see my true vocation was being a forensic pathologist or a detective, and with the police force still a Catholic boys' club and medicine out of the question, naturopathy looked the nearest I'd get. Why were they forever talking about what was wrong with them? Treating symptoms instead of causes?

Physics and chemistry were still boysy, nothing useful like how to stop mayonnaise curdling or why salt lowers the boiling point of water. The best part was reading Jacques Monod, that everything in the universe is the fruit of chance and necessity, and Arthur Koestler's *The Case of the Midwife Toad*, which argues for the inheritance of acquired characteristics. The day Denis Stewart, the botany lecturer, took us to Gosford to forage in railway cuttings for echinacea and valerian was pretty good too, though I attributed that to the survival of the Royal

Apothecaries' genes, never dreaming that in Dorset it's days like this that are setting Christopher Hitchens on the road to atheism.

But like all minority groups naturopathy was beset by the usual schism, traditionalists versus modernists, who naturally won and put up the fees.

One of our guest lecturers had been Dr Bill Vayda, an orthomolecular nutritionist. A much-married Hungarian who wanted to be an Italian, he wasn't comfortable writing English, so for two years I sat at his kitchen table in Paddington, cutting and pasting stories, mostly from *Scientific American* and the *Journal of the American Medical Association*, linking them with folksy passages to create *Health for Life: Are You Allergic to the Twentieth Century?* If Bill didn't have a patient, he'd come in and talk about the bigger evolutionary picture, how agriculture, ie waving fields of wheat, had been invented only five minutes ago, and until a few seconds ago anyone allergic to gluten had probably died in infancy before there was any question of bequeathing anything, genetically or otherwise.

In the 1960s coeliac disease had been something that only happened in America. Cows' milk had long been a culprit – at naturopathic college, Mrs Thatcher's abolition of free school milk was seen as her noblest achievement. But now there were peanuts, dander (how tragic, to be allergic to horses!) and not just hens' and ducks' eggs but those of innumerable microscopic things breeding in mattresses and pillows, so you'd have to buy new ones every year or so. Clearly I'd led a charmed life, not that it helped. Like the psychic business it was another cross to bear; they'd assume I was deeply spiritual, only ever shopping in health food stores (as if I could afford it!) and opposed to modern medical science, when I wasn't. Or only when it was opposed to me.

Placental lamb injections, which presidents and dictators,

maybe even Popes, were now having in Swiss clinics, were banned by the AMA, but when *Cosmopolitan* discovered it could be done in Fiji, I didn't mind a bit spending a week at a luxury resort sharing five minutes of pain with Maggie the model. With the wrong sort of Irish genes, an Australian woman can wind up looking sixty by the time she's forty, too, like Cardinal Pell or Bob Ellis, with a face like an unmade bed

Contact lens changed from glass to plastic, but Cousin Deirdre, and of course my mother, were still telling me I looked better in glasses. I suspect Deirdre was worried it'd encourage her husband, who was all for progress. I remember her cutting up a Savoy cabbage for coleslaw as early as 1954 when every cabbage's destiny was to be boiled to smithereens. But after *Women in Love* in 1969, bloody Ken Russell, when any man wanted to discuss D H Lawrence you knew it was time to run, you could read his mind only too well.

Another medical discovery was that if you loved God enough you could beat cancer, but after dear old Mina survived a second mastectomy, for once the family agreed with me, hating the Pope enough, and the government, probably worked just as well.

***

In Nick's final year of high school the kid and I moved, along with Yoshinori and Artemis the cat, into my first house, a tiny two-up two-down terrace built to accommodate warders at the old Darlinghurst Goal. By late November Nick was there too, until he left for England in May. Don't ask how we managed, or how I got a mortgage either, I suspect banks still had an old boys' system (as well as Uncle Tom, a long-dead Uncle Eric had also been a manager).

I bought a food processor and thanks to *Trading Post*, a Wilhelmine walnut piano with a half-iron frame from a Mrs Lipari in Marrickville, with rather worn felts and only a few cigarette burns. And my kitchen renovation was a success exceeding the bounds of probability, as it was still there as late as 2010 after at least two gay owners had put in a spa, polished floors and the tiled Art Nouveau fireplace I could only dream about. Besides, I'd had other obligations.

Back then Steve wasn't exceptional, unless they were very young, like his two nieces learning Greek dancing, ethnics didn't want to know about their cultural heritage. So the kid and I went to Ikaria with Savoula, the mother of a gay friend, who'd left twenty-five years ago. Her mother still lived there, and no sooner had we schlepped our bags up from the quay to her tiny house than hostilities resumed. Luckily the kid and I were able to move to a tiny farmhouse in the mountains, with drystone walls and rabbit hutches, vacated by a relative. Or was it a friend? In Agi Kirikos it hardly mattered.

My Greek briefly bloomed, only to vanish forever, which I feared would happen with my French and German too – without Gerard Depardieu Australian grandmothers would be as monolingual as their grandchildren. If the government had been smart they'd have done a deal with Singapore Airlines and had a girl read the evening news in whichever Asian language was then deemed essential, with subtitles. That's another of their urban myths, introduce boys early enough, there's no problem, the kid and his mates adored *Fitzcarraldo* almost as much as they liked *Withnail and I.*

By now the big new thing was authenticity, and it's not every native speaker who understands the peculiarities of his own language, or is even aware they *are* peculiar. So language classes were all about speaking. Become as a little child, behold how they learn without pain at their mother's knee!

But I'm a grown woman, I want to know how a language works, the basic rules and where words, like anything else, have come from. Was a *baguette* once thinner, like a grissini, seeing it's the same word for a magician's wand or a conductor's baton? Why did Germans think *weib* pejorative – was it feminist bias, or social class as with fishwife, meaning a low foul-mouthed woman? Or indeed both?

That's how I met Jiri, in a coffee shop where I was recovering from an hour of aural water-boarding. He spoke perfect English, but with an accent so I could tell he'd left after puberty (the invaluable *New Scientist*) and pretty soon that he'd also been through the wars metaphorically. Whereas Max had driven me past apartment blocks in the Eastern Suburbs which would be finished by Christmas, because of the recession anything Jiri showed me was no longer his, neither was any part thereof, even the lovely house where he'd lived before the divorce.

You'd think it could have happened to any woman in my line of business, easy on the eye as we mostly were back then, and trained to record the lives of others. But it must have been another thing that was only happening in America, men who needed to talk about the literal war, which in Jiri's case had begun when Hitler, having engulfed the Sudetenland, devoured Bohemia and Moravia which on 16 March 1939, from Prague Castle, were proclaimed Protectorates of the Third Reich.

'I was about ten, just past playing with toy soldiers, standing the window watching them march down the street and thinking how splendid and purposeful they looked in their grey uniforms. A proper army, unlike our Czech soldiers in their red and green, who always reminded me of an operetta.'

As if we don't all make mistakes, and don't realise at the time what our mothers are crying about – the afternoon he'd seen her in the bluebell wood where she'd gone to pick mushrooms. And it's a safe bet that by 2011 anyone zipping around Prague Castle on Segways and doing merry re-enactments of St Vitus's dance wouldn't have known either, that when I was eleven, 'When did you last see your father?' was a little Cavalier boy in satin pants staring down an inquisitorial Puritan during the Civil War. Whereas now it became Jiri aged eleven, setting out on the tram with the bread his mother had baked that morning, intending to say he was sorry about whatever they'd argued over the last time (kings, or bishops or rooks) and expecting the same obliging guard. Coming back with the bread on his knee, impossible to conceal in a pocket, and his cheeks as hot as it had been when it came out of the oven.

At first it wasn't too bad, quite fun in fact listening to Jiri's lawyerly invective, but when his rage encompassed me, I wished Victor Bizannes had been there, just to make a few things clear.

Firstly, it is an accident of birth that my client is a subject of the British Empire. Nor can she be blamed for also being a foreign-born citizen of a boggy misbegotten country like Ireland.

Secondly, my client will produce evidence (Elgar's Cello Concerto, as tabled) that all Anglo-Saxon music is not jingoistic rubbish, vastly inferior to Dvorak, Smetana, and Janacek. She regrets referring to the Vltava as the Moldau, which was an isolated incident.

Thirdly, not once did my client deny that the Australian government, at the time in question composed entirely of said Anglo-Saxons and Irish, were capable of causing, by accident or design, the countless frustrations and humiliations your client claims he endured.

Finally, my client warmly concurred on numerous occasions, regarding pie floaters ('sorry, Your Honour, that's a pie swimming in pea soup, once popular in Adelaide'), the appalling coffee, rat-trap cheese, insipid sausages, and other things of a culinary nature.

But it wouldn't have helped. Jiri's problem wasn't one that

could be solved in a court of law, not that the evidence wasn't there, the way he'd take me to interview his old girlfriends, Martina who'd spent three years in an attic in Amsterdam, and Adele who'd always ask us to bring her vanilla slices from the patisserie in Plumer Road (the best in Sydney, she said) because that was what she'd craved most in Auschwitz. Even with rebirthing, another of their enthusiasms, his father would still have been among the drowned, when what Jiri wanted to be re-born literally, from some other womb which would have allowed him to remember too, like the ones who'd been saved.

***

So I'd never learnt to play chess. As I'd say to Jiri, did I *look* the sort of woman Australian men would waste good time on, let alone money, by inviting me to concerts and operas? Pretty confident he'd agree, not that I'm entirely blaming them, given the exorbitant price of culture the last thing Australian women needed was liberation. Luckily Cousin Ollie, the Aquarian who'd surprised the family by winning the concerto competition, was now with an orchestra, so I got lots of free tickets.

Exactly how Cousin Billy had died was unclear, but his tastes had already turned to poetry, because in 1965 he'd sent me Edith Sitwell's *Gardeners and Astronomers,* ('God knows *what* she's talking about, darl, but it sounds wonderful!') and added a few lines of his own. So Ollie had succeeded to the role of favourite cousin, which wasn't always easy now he was exercised not just about Papists but the imminent extinction of blue-eyed people. Given his conflicted relationship with his mother, dear old Mina, it was pretty foreseeable he'd relate to Percy Grainger, so it was just as well Ollie was ardently pro-circumcision, being convinced that Catholics weren't, never missing the opportunity to roll yet another cigarette and expound on the horrors he'd witnessed in Allora primary school.

Seeing Steve as an act of genetic betrayal, Ollie didn't want to hear about Greece, how on the *plataea,* every day around one o'clock two waiters would come out of a tavern, pick up a drunk sitting outside, chair and all, and carry him up the hill. They'd been doing it when she was a girl, Savoula said, taking him home to his mother's for lunch. As Agi Kirikos was full of people living to a ripe age, I'd figured they might be doing for it another twenty-five years and the Mediterranean diet was only half the story.

True, Hillary Clinton will later say 'it takes a village to raise a child', as if it all ends there, and you're never expected to carry them up hills when they've become drunken octogenarians, or even sober ones, let alone have them live under your own roof? Even if I'd never been near Ikaria, I'd still have liberated my mother, shortly after my return.

***

[42] Laestrygonians, a tribe of giant cannibals who menaced Odysseus on his homeward journey.

Chapter 13
Personal Best

Good better best, Never let it rest, Till your good is better,
And your better best. -Attributed to St Jerome

It was the best of times, it was the worst of times. A Tale of
Two Cities -Charles Dickens,

***

One thing I knew, Dickens knew enough good and bad times
to have a viable sample, not only familiar with roast goose and
turkey but understanding the entire process, the buying and
stuffing, the basting and timing and carving, about which I still
know as little as St Jerome. The only time I'd experienced a
proper Christmas, it was the best and worst simultaneously,
London snow deep'n'crispaneven, when the outrageously camp
actor Dibbs Mather whose boys were the same age as mine,
staged the full production.

So change might be paradoxical too, and when it's by human
agency, I figured there were only four ways it could go.

With luck, getting better; changing yet staying the same,
obviously more common, or the French wouldn't be saying *plus
ça change, plus c'est la même chose;*or achieving this
intentionally rather than inadvertently, which if you can believe
Guiseppe di Lampedusa requires ruthless Machiavellian planning
and is consequently extremely rare. But with the fourth the very
fact that Germans have a word for it, *verschlimmbessern*, to
make something worse by attempting to make it better, tells you
all you need to know, and that's the most charitable
interpretation of Pluto's perihelion phase, starting in 1979 when

it spent twenty years being the seventh instead of the eighth planet from the sun, a mere 4.44 billion km away instead of 7.38 billion at aphelion, which correlated with changes nobody could have predicted. That by 1999 St Jerome's six beloved babies, good, better, best and their antonyms, would have been disappeared, the old dead poets and the proverbs too, and even the sun itself, after a lifetime of veneration, regarded with fear and loathing.

***

It had been April 1980 when my mother moved in, so it looked like the macrocosm hadn't had any long-term transformational agendas, like after ten or twenty years we'd realise we truly loved each other, because within three months she was dead.

It was more like Ted used to tell me about going to see Wal's marriage guidance woman, I'd shown good intent and been let off lightly. Just as my mother had been, after taking her beloved boys to lunch, probably at David Jones's, and minutes after the small final triumph of completing the cryptic crossword. Perhaps it was the same phenomenon the general practitioners told me about, happy emotional events triggered exits as well as entrances.

It started with a sudden thump upstairs in the middle bedroom, around nine-thirty, waking the kid who was now sleeping in a corner of mine. Yoyo had gone home to Shizuoka City and it was Sophie from Seoul who helped me lift her onto the bed.

Once I'd been going to have a Sophie of my own who'd play flawless Bach fugues from the *Anna Magdalena Klavierbuch*. Not that I ever told the psychotherapist, how I'd interviewed some doctor who'd persuaded me to switch to a contraceptive pill called Sequens. She wouldn't have believed in medical misadventure, and by now they didn't either, you went into hospital with an ingrowing toenail and came out minus a leg, you must have *wanted* to be an amputee. You were always in control of your life, they said.

The only comfort I'd ever found was *The Tibetan Book of the Dead,* how a departed soul hovers awaiting a suitable opportunity, unless the death has been violent or untoward, when it can become impatient and not realise its mistake until a few months later.

Sophie and I stood there trying not to watch each other watching her, waiting for the kid to come back with my compact. Another Hollywood tradition, like sending expectant fathers to boil gallons of water.

'Is she dead yet?'

One thing was certain, the kid was hoping she was, this interloper who claimed she couldn't read to him, yet never failed to notice when he was naughty. It's not easy, explaining macular degeneration and peripheral vision to a four year old.

The gurgle grew steadily fainter, and then ceased. On the bedside table the little red clock ticked on beside the completed crossword. Was Sophie a Buddhist? With lodgers, I didn't always ask, so bringing up *The Tibetan Book of the Dead* might be like asking Hindus about Ayurvedic medicine, or Chinese about acupuncture. What if she were a Christian, fell to her knees and expected me to pray along to Jesus?

Giving Sophie twenty dollars and sending her up to the pub for a bottle of brandy was the last time that night I was in control of anything. It's a wonder they even considered me capable of telling when someone's dead. The next step was to phone the 'contractors', another of their sinister euphemisms, so before long two men, the size of plainclothes detectives but less worldly, arrived. Again I asked why – she'd had angina episodes for years, couldn't it wait until tomorrow when I could talk to her doctor?

They looked uncomfortable and mumbled about bodily fluids, so it was impossible not to laugh, remembering *Dr Strangelove*, and again at whatever euphemism they used for corpse, which they took downstairs in a zippered plastic bag, knocking askew the Margaret Preston lithographs of the red ranunculi like the ones she'd grown in Eumundi.

I imagined them driving off into the night, shaking their heads and wondering where some people were brought up.

The exceptionally cold winter meant heaps of homeless people found dead in parks and under bridges who had to be autopsied first, so the funeral wasn't for weeks. Kinsela's, with its beautiful Art Deco light fixtures and glass doors, hadn't yet become a nightclub, and in the viewing room I walked straight past her, mistaking her for an old man, which the Maltese funeral director said happened all the time, at the end of life the sexes look much the same, like newborn babies. So that was definitely good, discussing T S Eliot with total strangers isn't something that happens too often.

***

At *Woman's Day* Epping had been beyond the boundaries of the known world, so I was ill-equipped to tell what kind of people lived in the desirable brick residences with the pools and purple tibouchina trees, except that they took God and country pretty seriously, Australian flags fluttering and resplendent new churches of which some were Seventh Day Adventist, the faith of my new employers, the Wards, who were planning a monthly health magazine and needed an editor. It sounded pretty good, only having to drive to Epping on Fridays, and I'd already interviewed an Adventist couple living somewhere even more remote, where I'd seen my first fax machine. My editor at *Pol,* Rob Ingram, came up with one of his usual nifty captions, *The Electronic Cottage*. It wasn't something our place was going to turn into any time soon.

The Osborne computer spent its first weeks on my dining-room table, miffed at people mistaking it for a portable sewing machine and thrumming its fingers while it waited for me to divorce the IBM golfball. I already felt terrible, even girlfriends who'd never touched a typewriter (which many educated women saw as shamefully secretarial) recalled their long and faithful service to literature, whereas computers were alien slouching beasts, the ally of commerce and teenage boys.

I tried explaining that the Adventists' enthusiasm for technology and self-employment was also about being in control of your life, where there's no separation of church and state you never know when they'll conscript you or tax you in the cause of some holy war, leaving less money for tithing. The last person I'd heard mention tithing was Max, who hadn't seemed worried about the Queen and the Archbishop of Canterbury plunging Australia into foreign conflicts.

The Wards also published newsletters on small business and tax minimisation, for which I wrote extra stories about how to stay healthy in body and mind, and wealthy too – the office was full of books like *The Dynamic Laws of Prosperity* and Napoleon Hill's *Think and Grow Rich*. Not that anything seemed to work with the kid. He simply didn't pay attention, or as Sydney Grammar Prep put it, 'a tad vague but so sweet, a delight to have in the class'.

Phil Wards's mother, the accountant, was always up for a chat about how it's less stressful living with people who share your values, but there was also a journalist called Loell, who wore black silk shirts and aftershave, things not usually associated with God-fearing vegetarians.

'It's easier for Jews,' he'd say, deadpan. 'They're allowed to be talented and glamorous'.

'Imagine if you were Amish,' I'd say.

***

Not many women approved of Bob either, though unlike the computer he hadn't been a total surprise. Back in the Fifties, one of the Somerville House girls had got a scholarship to the States, and married a divorced Presbyterian. But now she'd written to say they were coming back and would everyone please be nice to Bob until she and the kids arrived.

Bob was an engineer who'd moved into selling manufacturing systems, he wasn't into literature and art house cinemas, and made heartless jokes as only New Yorkers can. The only Presbyterian had been his father, who'd come from Northern Ireland and clearly wasn't responsible for him looking like Gene Wilder on the way to Isaac Bashevis Singer. So it soon wound up being just Ruth (the girl on the train I'd 'bonded with' in Orientation Week) and me inviting lonesome Bob to home-cooked dinners, and going up to his rented place at Newport.

Is it my fault I don't get sunburnt, or seasick in dinghies? Or not allergic to mercury – Bob adored fish restaurants. So soon it's just me having suntan oil rubbed on her back, and eventually, in the spa, feeling his hand slowly but surely creeping down. I'm hardly breaking up his marriage, it was broke already, he said, and before long I was seeing why. He wasn't lying about moving out either.

Apart from being amusing, something I'd never associated with ex-marines, Bob was the only man I ever met who understood what I still regard as men's business. How shocked I'd been in the Fifties by those cartoons in garages and electrical repair shops – 'This is the car/toaster/wiring Dad tried to fix!' And by now, anywhere else, it was 'fix the fucking thing yourself, you're a feminist, aren't you?'

Naturally Bob had downsides, he hated Ay-rab food, anything

from Claudia Roden was out apart from falafels, he even spread butter on pappadums. His mother came from Bialystock, which also takes a hundred years to get over.

'You see any *schwartzes* around here, kid? Any servants waiting for us to put our knives and forks together, so they can tell we're finished? For crissakes, Sadie, it's the twentieth century!'

The only person who approved of Bob was Ollie. Those big blue eyes, if only we could breed!

***

By now Phil Ward was so preoccupied he'd have okayed a trip to the moon, never mind a nutrition conference in Miami. The Hotel Doral served shrimp starters you couldn't jump over. 'You see any starving children here?' I said, but irony was long dead, and at breakfast the same people who'd given papers about obese Zunis and Hopis would be demolishing every iced and sugary roll in the breadbasket. What better excuse to visit Charleston, which apart from the Dock Street Theatre (*Porgy and Bess!*) had the fattest black people in America? In the Veterans' Hospital there was one who'd had to be lifted off his porch with a crane, diamond-shaped and dribbling over the sides of the bed like an inflated stingray.

For centuries it's been necessary for Irish families to ship their surplus sons off somewhere, and as everyone I found in the Charleston phone book said the best person to ask was Jewell, I drove one hundred miles to a place called Zwanzig because it's twenty miles from somewhere else where freckly boys drink grape soda and look straight out of a Norman Rockwell calendar. And next thing I'm sitting at the kitchen table, eating okra I've just helped pick, looking at Jewell's husband Jimmy who looks exactly like my Uncle Colin in Warwick.

Sunday morning Jewell drove me to see the Baptist church

154

they normally went to, which like all the others, even black people's, might have been painted only yesterday. If my newfound kin approved of invading wherever it was that year, Lebanon? they never said. The only war I heard about was the one Americans still haven't got over, when Jewell's mother came to lunch and remembered her mother's stories, how they'd buried the silver in the garden before the Yankees came, and after they'd gone a fifteen year old aunt called Fevery, like the ones in the family graveyard Jewell had shown me, was never seen again.

***

In Johannesburg I'd winced when people said give them a hand and they want the whole arm - when there's a black hand right under your nose, serving lunch, decent people say it in French. Possibly it's why, fifteen years later in Australia, there was now no way they'd believe it was the same with dingoes. I'd be lucky to reach the supermarket checkout or survive a bus trip without someone telling me of course Lindy was guilty, you only had to look at her, and everyone knew Seventh Day Adventists drank their own urine. The only laugh I'd get all week was Fridays at Epping, if Phil was away in Alice Springs.

'He's looking for that talking dingo again', Loell would say.

Not that we didn't hope he'd find one. But where was everyone else, not a single Zola to write *J'accuse*!? What had happened to being on the side of the underdog? A few years earlier I'd taken the boys to see *Zulu Dawn*, and some woman behind me was going on about the only good nigger being a dead one.

'Belt up,' I told her.

'Go back where you came from,' she replied - it must have been my still-Englishy voice or she was the sort who, had we been formally introduced, would have looked twice at my nose and said 'but what was your name *before*?' You expect teenage boys to want to crawl under their seats when their mother causes a commotion, usherettes racing up with torches, but it was beyond wincing, all those women coming up afterwards saying they were so pleased I'd spoken up, they'd been just going to.

***

The early Eighties saw another change in my close personal relationships. Dr Simpson retired to spend more time growing bonsais in back molars, so instead of hearing about calcium deficiency in Japan, I was now listening to Michael about Johannesburg.

'Oh, you're so *brave*', he'd say, 'all my other patients would want an injection', when it was just some piffling filling. So to make his day a bit more exciting I'd tell him how when I was a kid there was a war on, no dentists, and any loose tooth just got the string-and-doorknob treatment. He said his grandparents remembered the same in Latvia, and being dosed every spring on molasses and sulphur, though that too had only ever happened to Ian and Sheila, and only according to dear old Mina, who was now telling me my mother only married my father on the rebound, and because she felt sorry for his two motherless children.

***

Arthur Dignam (*The Thinking Woman's Sex Object*) who'd played Brother Francine in *The Devil's Playground*, had a love-child too, Nicholas Gledhill, who'd just beaten the kid for the role of PS in *Careful He Might Hear You*. I was trying for a film career myself, heartened by Bruce Beresford's *Breaker Morant* and *Tender Mercies*, and Peter Wier's *Picnic at Hanging Rock*, and the Australian Film Commission was flinging money at women for creative script development.

The script editors, most of them Muscovines or failed Marxist schoolteachers, mostly lived in Balmain and were intent on

156

avoiding stereotypes. 'You must have done a lot of research', one of them said, about my script set in Queensland country town in WW2. Maybe I didn't look, or sound, like her idea of someone who could milk a cow and believed in water divining. As for men like Jiri, what would a property developer in the Eastern Suburbs know about suffering?

***

'Sadie, you've gotta lie, cheat and steal to survive!' Bob said, but if I'd lied I'd never have been hired by *Today's Computers* ahead of a hundred and fifty applicants. I didn't know that until Ken McGregor, the editor, told me over lunch that he'd wanted a woman who didn't know diddly squat, because a man would pretend he did and readers would end up none the wiser.

Every day I asked questions, of suited people in tall glass office blocks, about things I hadn't known existed when I'd got out of bed, and then told them I didn't understand the answers, even when they weren't from India or South Africa or Kansas. Some days I didn't even understand Ken, but the Big Six turned out not to be footballers but accountancy firms who were now expanding into management consulting, where thanks to the Seventh Day Adventists I felt much more comfortable.

Besides, I'd just reviewed Dave Barry's *Claw Your Way to the Top; How to Become The Head of a Major Corporation in Roughly a Week.* It had a cartoon of a bemused woman in an apron, with a caption, '*so you think you only know how to make tuna casserole*?' Meaning mothers were already experts at multi-tasking, negotiating, prioritising, forward planning and worst-case scenarios. Even if the health professionals disagreed.

I don't think Bob was right there either, 'Sadie, you oughta nail that goddam kid's ass to the wall,' when he'd go missing for hours and have to be retrieved from whichever supermarket carpark skateboarders favoured. But it was better than hearing how I was too hard on him, he'd promised not to do it again, such a lovely boy, he'd grow out it.

***

By now the celebrity planet was Chiron, named for the wounded and exceptionally wise centaur, who in no time they'd transformed into Persephone. [43] But although Chiron was a mere speck in the macrocosm, in the microcosm it grew ever bigger, every second woman and not a few men, whether or not they'd ever heard of either of them, imagining themselves grievously wounded and insightful, and thus best suited to heal the wounds of others, whether they had them or not.

We Old Believers, who also held that one's identity depended not on the month but on the precise minute of departure/arrival, wanted no truck with it, but regarding the endemic spread there was now some scientific basis, the Hundredth Monkey Effect, whereby a learned behaviour, in any species, spreads like wildfire once it reaches a critical mass [44] With a species who can read and watch television, it'd take no time at all.

***

In 1985 Nick and Janine returned from three years of roaming and opened the Drawing Room on Crown Street. For weeks I never dared drive past it at night, lest my heart be broken by seeing it totally empty, all those crisp white tables and sparkling wine glasses set out with such hope, but it soon got good reviews. In its former life it had been a gay bookstore offering special services upstairs, accounting for the hooks in the ceiling where Janine and I hung mobiles of May Gibbs' Gumnut Babies, Snugglepot and Cuddlepie, and by July 1986, shortly after their wedding in the park, I'm the grandmother of Nichola Frances Josephine, named for the two midwives. Otherwise I'd have made a strong case for Audacia, there must have been one somewhere in a Victorian novel.

Karl's wedding, to Fiona in April 1987, was strictly traditional, though I think they too had Kahlil Gibran. Wal and I managed a civil hello, but from then on it was as if each of us had become invisible to the other, and it's unlikely I'd have been any different if I'd known. The only time he'd ever mentioned death it was going to be self-inflicted, when he'd sing his version of Billie Holiday, *I'm gonna cut my throat and throw away my head.* And even if he'd known, and I *had* been all forgiving and mellow, I doubt he'd have been any different from that day in the registry office, 'don't be fucking *ridiculous'*.

At my father's funeral, a Brown or a Jones would have been understandable, not Rudolph instead of Randolph, triggering stifled giggles. I hadn't yet discovered Rebbe Nachman – 'you call *this* bad?' says God. 'I'll show you what bad really is'.

After his retirement, Wal had found the perfect second career as a ship's photographer and it was some parson who'd got to know him on luxury Pacific cruises. Yet every time he'd embark on some amusing anecdote, it was why he'd never forget Walter *Greenfield*, everyone's jaws dropping in disbelief, the boys and me on one side of the aisle and Glenda and what remained of *Woman's Day* on the other, thinking maybe there's a life after death after all, Wal still exercising his black sense of humour.

My ex-mother-in-law had died while I was in London, but at some stage she'd told my mother she'd always believed her father, whose initial point of arrival had been Guernsey, on Christmas Day 1872, was Jewish. And somewhere in those last four months, maybe at the second-hand furniture place (my mother insisting she's become accustomed to a single bed), or while I'm driving over the Bridge at peak hour, my mother told me, which suggested that Mrs. Rosenberg and I, on those mornings at the Jewish Historical Society, were on the right track. The wedding in the Methodist church, to which neither the groom (draper, of East Maitland) nor the pregnant bride (spinster, of West Maitland) belonged and where the only witnesses were the minister's wife and a Mrs Euphemia Harris, whom we suspected was his boss.

By the next century there'll be a photograph, at what looks like some formal occasion, showing a darkly handsome young man with soulful eyes whom older women might well tend to indulge, but they're that smart, how come she'd hire the son of a labourer when there must have been dozens of other young men in East Maitland more familiar with lace and dimity?

***

[43] Discovered in 1977 by Charles T Kowal, but possibly sighted as early as 1895.

[44] Lawrence Blair, *Rhythms of Vision: The Changing Patterns of Belief*, Croon Helm, London,1976; Lyall Watson, *Lifetide: a Biology of the Unconscious,* Hodder & Stoughton, London, 1979.

Chapter 14
Greed is Good to Me

The point is, ladies and gentlemen that greed, for lack of a better word, is good. -Gordon Gekko/Michael Douglas in *Wall Street*

***

By now they'd become entranced with chaos theory, that one flutter of a butterfly's wing could cause a hurricane, so maybe that explains how and why the Nineties started halfway through the Eighties, when all those geeky boys in Silicon Valley, now enormously rich, caused thousands of Australian mothers to be snatched up like Dorothy/Judy Garland and whirled into the corporate world, to find it was they, the tuna casserole bakers, who were the wizards now – all those things boys need reminding about, if they were ever told in the first place.

Today's Computers was soon taken over but Ron Plater, looking not a day older than when he'd been a sub-editor at the *Courier-Mail,* had a new client, the University of NSW's Graduate School of Management. Ron worked from home, a historic stone cottage in Darling Point where I spent three days a week persuading graduates that what they needed to claw their way to the top was an MBA.

Editors couldn't get enough of women who'd found it worked wonders for self-esteem, especially post-divorce, though I persuaded *Time Magazine* it could also be romantic – Jerry Liossatos, who'd put Elpis through the Franz Liszt Academy, and now she was a concert pianist she was returning the favour. Thank goodness for foreigners! But by now I rarely met the old sort who'd widened my horizons and told jokes about Sean Ferguson. It was their children, needing to remember everything. And next thing it's Michael Douglas in his red braces telling the world that greed is good, definitely what they want to hear, not that Tom Wolfe has just written *The Bonfire of the Vanities*.

Every morning I suited up, choosing from several designer blouses and remembering the good shoes for after I'd walked down across Hyde Park in my Reeboks, when I'd stop being foolish Mrs Smith, uneducated single mother who'd been reading too many books, (and might herself be mentally ill) and transform into staff writer, Management and Professions, at *Australian Business,* taken to lunch every day in fashionable restaurants by PRs, lawyers and management consultants.

Julie McBeth was my counterpart at the opposition, *Business Review Weekly,* but I didn't know she was one of us until the next century, in a draughty Melbourne convent in the coffee break between Hellenic philosophers and financial forecasting. We wondered how we'd ever stood it, pretending to be enthralled by cross-vesting and offshore tax havens.

At *Australian Business* it was often a steep learning curve linguistically, realising cross-vesting wasn't about transvestite judges, and that exposure no longer involved dirty old men in raincoats. And being a male universe, English was still peppered with sporting metaphors, level playing fields and changing goalposts, only now it was a whole new ballgame, where Bob filled me in on eightballs and catbird seats, and when I'd lucked out as opposed to in, like getting all those terrific books to review, Charles Handy's (go Ireland!) *The Gods of Management,* and the one about the boiling frog, and Allan Bloom's *The Closing of the American Mind*.

Forum, Cosmo, and *Cosmopolitan* had changed men to some extent, but male journalists still hankered to write about exciting stuff – takeovers, financial crises, blood on the boardroom carpet – and be courted by wicked capitalists their fathers would have strung from a lamppost. So I was largely free to decide how to fill my three pages per week of what they still saw as women's business. Organisational behaviour and human resources, how to delegate, hire and fire, make succession plans and prepare for contingencies, which now they'd become addicted to positive thinking were increasingly likely. (What had happened to yin and yang? How could you have constant growth?) In other words, everything they'd have known already if only they'd got over their hang-ups about servants and child labour, though ten years later, watching South Park, I could see those gnomes who steal underpants (Point 1) to get rich (Point 3) and forget Point 2 were a worldwide phenomenon.

People faced with a camera no longer said cheese, let alone *petit pois*. They said money, and for the Collectibles pages I wrote about what they could spend it on, visible and tangible things like Ermenegildo Zegna suits, Louis Vuitton luggage and Abercrombie and Fitch leisurewear reflecting their lifestyles, and every so often about luxury health spas and collagen implants which required road testing.

But one day it wasn't steamed mussels and sautéed duck breasts with lawyers and management consultants, at Edna's Table or Machiavelli's or the Intercontinental, but lunch with a journalist turned PR I'd known back in our tuna casserole days when we'd had husbands. And suddenly I stop, a forkful of John Dory halfway to my mouth, because she's reminding me of some other woman in another restaurant, light years ago at a book launch, whose husband suddenly enters looking as if he's achieved one homicide already, because he's shaved with an unsteady hand, shouting 'Where's your fucking Jewish lover?'

'You *must* remember. I helped you escape through the

kitchen, out to the car park.'

'Sandy, are you *sure?*'

Her ex was now a famous novelist, maybe a talent for fiction was acquirable through osmosis.

'I've never seen you so terrified.'

Still, when someone's put themselves out for you, it's ungracious not to remember, even if you'd prefer to *vergessen*, and we soon went back to discussing employee share schemes, having another chardonnay and becoming deliciously uncertain about puddings. It was a restaurant called Fishwives in Surry Hills, now long gone. I don't mind remembering that.

***

I'd been right about cape gooseberries; one day at the American Club there were six or so flanking a chunk of Brie. Another new big thing was boardroom lunches and one day I went with Peter Fish, the Collectibles editor, to Clayton Utz, who were big in divorce and had several ferocious women, who favoured silky floral dresses and longish rolled hair, like French Resistance heroines. Well, they would, wouldn't they, after Glenn Close boiled that bunny in *Fatal Attraction* the last thing an erring husband needed was some ball-breaker in a suit.

The lawyers asked how practice management worked at our place, how many support staff did we have? One, we told them, a little shamefaced, after figuring out they meant secretaries. Already lawyers lived on a different planet.

Apart from Sue who supported Roger Johnstone the editor and Trevor Sykes the managing editor, the only person I could talk to about the greater scheme of things was Andrew who compiled the annual Rich List. The Berlin Wall and the Evil Empire crumbling, Nelson Mandela freed after twenty-seven years, were these the harbingers of further collapse of seemingly permanent structures?

Trevor Sykes, who wrote the Pierpont stock exchange column, would have known about Kondratiev cycles and Elliot Wave theories, too, maybe even Fibonacci sequences, but Trevor wasn't a sensitive New Age man. Most Friday afternoons he'd erupt from his office, rampaging past to grab some hapless bloke while the rest of us kept our heads down in case he'd decide we too were as useless as tits on a bull. If the kid had dropped in after school, from St Andrews, I'd stuff him in a metal clothes locker, in case visiting offspring were frowned upon.

Some Fridays Trevor was merely ebullient, which wasn't much better as he once attempted to waltz me around the floor, and spontaneous public dancing is yet another thing I didn't, as they now said, do.

***

I was luckier than Julie at *Business Review Weekly* – we had the Hyde Park Club downstairs where I'd swim a few laps after lunch and then drift off in a banana chair, knowing I could always claim I'd been meditating, another New Age thing Human Resource departments had embraced. I'd make an effort, but my mind invariably scurried off, hunting and retrieving mundane facts. How much did those exotic French knickers cost, the ones I'd seen on high-powered women in the change room? Should I buy a pair for when the lovely Englishman came back? Of course he would – plenty of people claimed to know about reviving moribund companies, but he'd actually walked the talk, with some brewery in the Midlands.

The day I'd interviewed him at the motel (the one where Pete Seeger once sat on the lawn and thrilled us with *Little Boxes*) he'd been in the pool, and after a while made an excuse about showering, emerging in a towel which he let slip while consulting me. Which antipodean insect did *loov* think was responsible for the red mark on his inner thigh? *Lady Chatterley's Lover* at last made sense. But within the hour he was due to be keynote speaker somewhere, so I thought of Mrs Thatcher and went right on asking about redundancy packages and Just-in-Time inventories, remembering that golden rule of management, if a thing's worth doing, it's worth doing properly.

***

Ever since the Sixties they'd been stealing our ancient wisdom, claiming the mid-life crisis was yet another amazing psychological discovery and it was now statistically proven, or so HR directors would tell me, that the mean age for executives and law partners quitting to start antique shops or ostrich farms was forty-two and a half. I still hadn't got around to Dante in the dark forest halfway through the journey of life, but thanks to *Pol* I'd learnt a lot about midlife crises, the day at Nimbin when I'd gone to interview Dr Ron Farmer, Tina Arndt's old mentor from the University of NSW, and he'd turned up stark naked on a tractor
[45]

It was February and the kid and I had just slogged up a leech-infested gully, so I took off my shirt and sat on the steps of his half-completed geodesic house, to hear why he'd not only abandoned academe but completely changed his views on masturbation. At puberty it's the worst thing boys can do, he told me as he nibbled sunflower seeds, it drains zinc from their brains. So the Victorians had been right after all, just as well I'd brought two tins of smoked oysters as well as the now-warmish white wine.

HR people also set much store by the Myers-Briggs Personality Inventory, or more recent variants of Jung's four types involving a circle divided into four. Hippocrates occasionally got a guernsey, (ancient Greeks were respectable, they'd invented democracy) but everyone's goal was to get in the top right-hand quadrant, to show they were innovative thinkers and born entrepreneurs, the very embodiment of the Aquarian Age.

'Bollocks', said the lovely Englishman, 'it's only about two percent of the population who are INTJs.[46] Not that it wasn't kind of flattering. They can identify with us all they like, but being born between 21 January and 18 February isn't nearly good enough, it's like claiming you're French because you were born in Paris. Or there'd need to be supporting evidence, close family, as it were, also resident in France, and although Mercury and Venus can never be more than twenty-eight and forty-eight degrees, respectively, from the sun in either direction, there's a high chance they're weren't, on the day.

I tried asking Ollie to work out the precise odds, admittedly he's good with computers and technology, but he just kept watching, for the umpteenth time, his video of Jacqueline du Pré playing the Elgar and insisting he's an atheist. As if that's a remotely rational excuse for not being interested in the workings of the solar system, or the wider applications of the Pareto principle, what they were now calling 'systems thinking', that there is no one root cause or rotten apple, because everything is connected and interdependent.

The people who took me to lunch were always saying eighty percent of a business comes from twenty percent of its customers, but the lovely Englishman was the only person who ever told me it's because in 1906 Vilfredo Pareto, the economist, discovered twenty percent of Italians owned eighty percent of the land, and then found it applied to all sorts of things, including the productivity of peas. Had Mendel noticed it too, in his monastery garden? They hadn't dared mention genetics for decades.

We'd lie in bed amusing ourselves by inventing coming up with variations, the way you do with Clausewitz's hypothesis, 'war is a continuation of politics by other means' though by now they were all into Sun Tze's *Art of War* and it's only later I start thinking the Aquarian Age is turning out to be twenty percent of the world making the other eighty percent do something they don't want to. Little by little, innovation was good only in hindsight, after a bright idea or intelligent guess had paid off, and being right one time out of ten or twenty was unacceptable, you had to be right all the time.

Assume makes an ass out of you and me!

That must have been why they started speaking in the middle passive voice; 'a program was implemented', 'a sustainable outcome was achieved', 'bombs fell'. Never anything that could get them into trouble, castrated or devoured.

***

When I scored a contra deal with British Airways to write about their management schools and hotels, I took the kid so I could show him the Tate and the Louvre, though there was little sign of him being uniquely artistically gifted like the ones they were forever writing about. Like any fifteen year old he kept creeping up from cattle class, past the dozing white-robed sheiks (it was Ramadan), desperate for a sliver of my Aylesbury duckling or *tarte aux abricots*. There was a free side trip too, to a European capital of your choice, so I chose Spain, for the Prado and in case Basil Fawlty hadn't been joking about Franco exterminating the rats. Like Mussolini, he must have got a few things right.

But the Goyas were away on loan, and the only good thing was being laid low with a cold, otherwise it would have been me paying for the kid's lunches and dinners, and not the Malaysian Tiger Woman next door who'd befriended him on the plane. (Do they normally stay in no-star pensions?).

We drove to Lisbon where some PR firm had a client, Taylor, Fladgate and Yeatman the port shippers, who'd fly us to Oporto, where one good thing Salazar did, admittedly inadvertently, was to cause people to flee to Brazil and abandon lovely eighteenth century mansions like the one which was now their head office. The Yeatman was a relative of the one who'd written *1066 and All That,* so at lunch we recalled even more Good Things, while the kid looked bemused and snaffled the last of the custard tarts. [47]

But it only made it worse, I came back and turned into Basil Fawlty, enraged that Australia still hadn't discovered *strapontins,* and still expected supermarket cashiers to stand up. How snobbish can you get, though by the next century, the *Washington Post* figures it's because Americans don't believe people are really working if they're sitting down.[48] Was it already mostly small brownish women? Sometimes I'd ask if there wasn't a union, only to be told it didn't worry them, they were used to it. It didn't seem to worry anyone else either, quite the contrary, the new big thing was *maquiladoras,* factories in Mexico with small brownish women they'd never need to see at all. What they called outsourcing.

***

Now that nine out of ten women had discovered their inner goddess was Persephone, the really Good Thing was Camille Paglia saying she was a vampire – so it wasn't just me who'd wondered about those goitrous PreRaphaelite necks! To encourage the kid I'd already put that Dante Gabriel Rossetti poster, the one where she's dopily contemplating the fatal pomegranate, in the downstairs loo. You'd have thought there'd have been a flash of enlightenment but I was never in there long enough. (Their extraordinary custom of keeping a stack of reading matter in such places!) So it's ironic I never realised the kid was a male Persephone, itching to be carried off to a universe ruled by a god every bit as black as Pluto. A skateboard heaven called South Central Los Angeles.

Why couldn't I marry Bob so we could live in America?

'I don't know about that,' I'd say, sounding like Steve whenever I mentioned money, now he was married to the Muscovine. For one thing Bob hadn't asked me and worse, he no longer wanted to retire to Maine, with cheap lobsters, snowy Christmases and Thanksgivings where I'd finally get to grips with turkeys, but to Florida, to avoid income tax. You're thinking surely I could have persuaded him on both counts, but with a deaf father girls don't get much practice. Besides, after the trip I was a bit like Persephone myself, hankering to return to the upper realms.

***

Yoshinori, now a father of three, was still writing at Christmas, and at last I saw how it's possible to have a strawberry farm in the middle of suburbia – several lots under cultivation, or with greenhouses, surrounding the house where the Yagi family had lived for a thousand years. There was a humungous television showing wrestling, and soaps where we'd laugh, as Japanese do, at drunk men giggling and falling into fish ponds. Even Yoshinori's grandmother laughed. She was close to ninety, still tending the cabbages and tea bushes and living a little shed Yoshinori called 'my grandmother's office'. I wouldn't have minded something like that myself.

Jerry and Elpis Liossatos, the romantic couple from my MBA days, were now importing pianos, and friends of Father Merritt, an American Episcopalian priest who'd arrived in the 1930s and now lived in the mountains in what was once a charcoal-gatherer's hut. It was late November and freezing, every morning he'd be out chopping firewood, looking exactly like Tolstoy, and every night it was the best of times, settling down at the *kotatsu* (coffee table covered by a padded quilt, with a radiator underneath) drinking whisky and talking about things I couldn't have asked at Yoshinori's. Sleeping under old sepia photographs of his grandmother and the husband who'd gone to fight in China and never come back, before it all turned into WW2. What Father Merritt refers to as *the unfortunate interruption,* as if it were a mere blip.

***

During the siege of Leningrad, were they there too, old women still sharing precious bread with pigeons? By the Moika Canal, near the Yussopov Palace where Rasputin was murdered, there was one feeding ducks as well. The Neva is frozen into little peaks like beaten egg whites, and as we drive across it in the little tourist van, Elena the guide points out the Walrus swimmers chipping holes in the ice. The couple in the back said they'd seen them the day before.

'We figured it's so bad they musta bin trying to commit suicide'.

And next thing it's Elena, who's twice my size, falling on my shoulder and bursting into tears.

'Our parents lived with Communism for sixty years, believed it, breathed it, would have given their lives for it, and now everyone's laughing at us.'

At the Hermitage I'd have cried myself, needing my memory jogged about Jephthah's daughter, the Prodigal Son and why people embarked for Cythera, instead of being told the size of everything and how much it had cost to acquire and restore. But there's only a girl insisting that some painting which is clearly about Crete, scantily-clad youngsters leaping over a bull, could be English because the English used to have bull fighting. She knows because she went to Art College.

Whether the kid ever saw them, two weeks later, who knows? With fifteen-year-old boys there's no opportunity they won't seize to rebel, regardless of how incredibly artistically gifted they are, and how painful the consequences. It's only after I've returned alone from Heathrow on Christmas Eve, to a reverse charge phone call where I hear about the horrors of Russian hospitals, due to his developing an embarrassing male affliction for which he'll take years to forgive me, and how the Irish Embassy then put him, suitably labelled, on a train to Moscow, for which I'll take years to forgive *him*. The wicked waste, on someone who knows no more about Anna and Vronsky than the American girl, or the poor old Russians, knows about Minoan Crete.

I'd seen the future all right, and it wasn't working one bit.

***

[45]. Dr Ron Farmer became a follower of Sathya Sai Baba, and helped found Toogoolawa Schools to provide alternative education for boys who'd dropped out or been suspended

[46] Introverted iNtuitive Thinking Judging, one of the sixteen personality types created by Isabel Briggs Myers with the help of her mother, Katharine Briggs, from the theories of psychologist Carl Jung.

[47] W C Sellar and R J Yeatman, *1066 and All That: A Memorable History of England, comprising all the parts you can remember, including 103 Good Things, 5 Bad Kings and 2 Genuine Dates*, Methuen, London, 1930.

[48] *The Washington Post, Taking a Stand So That Others Might Sit*, 21 January 2007,

Chapter 15
Early 1990s: Downtime

I want to be with those who know secret things, or else alone.

-Rainer Maria Rilke

***

The one consolation, and a bleak one, about returning to Sydney was finding we'd been right about the crumbling structures – the recession we had to have, and no sign of other doors opening, or only on the non-material plane. I'd never have known Lubavitcher *rebbes* gave brilliant Kabbala classes if one of our people, Bettina Davis, hadn't lived in Bondi. That was another price of progress, butcher's shops disappearing, talk about paradox, the more empowered women became, the less they could handle harmless badinage, 'I like a nice breast myself, luv and thighs too, tender as me own heart'. Not that Bettina, being from London, didn't give as good as she got, and it was she who suggested that outside the Eastern Suburbs, they mightn't yet know about Lubavitchers and their glamorous Rebbetzin with the eleven kids.

The *Bulletin* had gone to the dogs all right. I'm sure Rob Ingram could have come up with something better than *Safe Sects*. And their next effort, *God's Children Go Co-Ed*, was hardly an improvement, because the Anglicans at Stroud had gone back to the future with the double monasteries of the eighth century, the Clare sisters living across the duck pond from the Franciscan brothers.

Sister Angela was a radical feminist who drove a tractor and was writing a book about Godde, but at the Benedictines' Mountain Pass Abbey it was more back to the past, eating freshly baked pumpkin muffins with Sister Hildegarde, who'd gone to St Rita's and said they'd gazed at us too on the Clayfield tram, thinking how lucky St Margaret's girls must be. There was even a hermit and though she performed some quite humble task, in a little cabin under the gumtrees, there were constant enquiries, often from prominent corporate women. How soon could they start?

So that wasn't just me, either, drawn to solitude and contemplation. Robyn Davidson, another St Margaret's girl, was now famous for leading a bunch of camels across Central Australia, but they'd seen it more as a noble feminist achievement, so I didn't read *Tracks* until years later, thinking well, it wasn't just dingos, they can't have understood wild camels either, that you'd have to put in a lot of hard yards first. Before you could even become a novice, Sister Hildegarde explained, there was a process called discernment, having to think it over for six months. And then you'd have to be RC to start with. Still, I had quite a bit of time for contemplation now I was just good friends with Bob, who was living with a woman who didn't mind retiring to Florida and taking her chances with the alligators, bent sheriffs and Jewish widows.

Cairns, where Nick now lived, was somewhere between Miami and South Carolina, luxury resorts and overweight people going to strange churches and giving their children strange names. I'd do grandmotherly things with Nichola, plait her blonde hair and admire her fairy princess dress. How soft and chubby her hand was, quite unlike a little boy's, when we'd walk along the beach, hoping a baby crocodile might emerge from the mangroves.

'You'd be my brave girl, wouldn't you? Give him a good

thump on the nose! Always remember they're more afraid of us than we are of them.'

It was as if nothing had ever gone wrong back at Rangers Road, the boys coming home from kindy, bringing me a sloppy mug of tea and asking 'has Sophie come undone yet'? The blood worse than ever and three days since my mother left for Darling Point to play bridge with Aunt Trudie's friends and wonder what happened to that nice Dalkeith boy from Inverary Downs. Standing at the door, giving a final touch to her good hat, telling me doctors made too much fuss nowadays.

But Sophie had been wiser than us all, and had already floated upwards to become some other woman's little girl, with trusting hands and a vulnerable body, so that I could be free too. It can't really have been her, that bloody thing like a tea bag falling on the floor

**

By the summer of 1993, I'm drinking beer with Jenny in the Top Pub, now transformed into Joe's Waterhole, recovering from what we'd driven up from Brisbane to see after reading the lifestyle pages. Stalls with New Age candles, crocheted green tree-frogs, and women in homemade Ye Olde dresses seated at spinning wheels outside whatever they were now calling Nick's Blue and White Café. If we'd made an effort, we could probably have found the gay poetry readings.

The beer wasn't entirely remedial, it was also paying homage, *respect* as they now said, though if my father could have seen the Top Pub that day he'd have ordered something stronger. Pokies, buffets with satay and Thai chicken, an ad over the bar for somebody's beer which had been *Helping Ugly People Get Laid* since whenever. The little Four X man in the big straw boater never got laid. If the ladies' parlour had survived, they'd have had women in there with their hair in rollers, shelling peas.

'When I was about four, my father stood me up on the bar to sing *Little Annie Rooney is My Sweetheart*. And then *At the Balalaika*.'

'And then your mother appeared, breathing fire and brimstone.'

We know all about each other's childhoods, Jenny and her parents under the dining-room table in Putney hearing the bombs fall, so maybe I'd ramped mine up a bit like I did with Michael about the sulphur and molasses.

They who control the past control the future, and now it appeared I had neither.

Hadn't the head of Religious Studies at the University of Sydney, Professor Jim Tulip, assured me I'd be welcomed with open arms? Taken me to lunch too, so it couldn't have been anything personal from the days at St Lucia when he'd run the Evangelical Union. More likely in an election year it wouldn't have looked good, admitting aged persons while school-leavers begged and busked in the streets.

Obviously it was time to continue my education by other means

***

At the Great Synagogue, for a *Pol* story called *'Pomp and Circumstance'* it had been marvellous, gazing down at the men waving palms fronds and myrtle branches. But Rob said there'd been rumblings, someone thought I'd been sending them up for being patriarchal. Luckily Bettina had been to the butchers again and seen a flyer about a new Orthodox rabbi from England. I went to visit him, pretending I was considering conversion.

'But wouldn't you miss Jesus?'

Oh dear, did I have to spell it out, that we too have our embarrassments, our own *baal teshuvahs?*

'Lots of Australians are more, well, English,' I say, torn between hoping he's remembering *Brideshead Revisited* and hoping he isn't, or not the part I am, Evelyn Waugh being snooty about the Jesuits' furniture, not that presbyteries can have been full of high chairs and stuffed toys. But within seconds he smiles, understanding perfectly and we move on to discussing fate and free will, and Rabbi Akiva's belief that the best protection is the constant performance of *mitzvoth,* the doing of good deeds.

Although we'd agreed that reconstructing my kitchen might be too high a price to pay, it wasn't long before I set out for Central Synagogue one Friday evening, wearing my green and white Hermes scarf (a gift from Alan the South African) and feeling like Chandler's tarantula on the angel cake as I settled down behind the wooden lattice. [49] It's a bit like Mass with Aunt Madeleine, gazing not at graven images but the men opposite, the older ones looking like the Baal Shem Tov, and the younger ones as if they might float over tiny houses at midnight, embracing pale girls. Snow fell past the windows, wolves howled in Old South Head Road.

Passover was approaching and the rabbi, who'd now switched to English, was explaining *chometz,* how it's essential to ensure not the tiniest trace remains. I could understand how anything containing leaven, symbolising pride, would have to go, but I'd been making falafels for years and Claudia Roden never said you had to put yeast or baking powder in the hummus as well. How could such a sloppy substance possibly lurk in the back of kitchen cupboards, find its way into pockets and down behind sofa cushions? Unless Jews ate lots of falafels.

***

Rabbi Franklin said it sounded like I had a Jewish soul already, but Temple Emanuel might be better, it'd be in English. I didn't mind too much, *nefesh* or not, I lacked the genes for tying a scarf undowdily, and there was *a capella* singing on Saturday mornings. The only visible Hebrew had a translation underneath, *Know Before Whom Thou Dost Stand*, which I liked too, reminding the *kehilah* not to become like wild animals which lose their fear of humans.

Community was a word I was hearing a lot now I was doing home care, they must have assumed nobody remembered any more what a proper one looked like, those small towns they're still telling us are such horrible places. It was like journalism used to be, except you didn't need Wal's Refrigerator Guide, in old people's houses it was a safe bet there'd be frozen chicken and vegetable pies. Not necessarily because they liked them but because eighty percent of them had dentures, or only twenty percent of their teeth.

I'd thaw the pies in the microwave and try to cheer them up with some of Rabbi Fox's Friday night jokes, the Jew shipwrecked on a desert island who'd built two synagogues, one to go to and one he wouldn't be seen dead in.

On Sundays Rabbi's Breakfasts were brilliant, all the bagels and lox you could eat, and no end of issues requiring discernment. Should the morning *Sh'ma* be recited when there is sufficient light to distinguish a friend from an enemy at a distance of four cubits? Or as Rabbi Meir maintained, a wolf from a dog – though in the opinion of Rabbi Eliezer it's when you can tell a green thread from a blue one. And it didn't end there, there were also several kinds of witches, only some of whom must be put to death.

Sometimes, though, it meant becoming a whole lot smarter very quickly, like the Czarist officer who buys the pickled herrings from the Jewish pedlar on the train. One morning it was Mosaic law, involving a girl who'd taken a sweater to the dry cleaners to be dyed black, how much compensation was due when it turned out purple? It largely hinged on what the wool in the sweater was worth and whether the dyeing amounted to value-adding.

'Why not just give it to a girlfriend who likes purple?' I asked. 'Doesn't it count as a *mitzvah?*'

'A secondhand sweater?!' cried Rabbi Fox, in mock alarm.

***

Months slid by, I learnt Sabbath blessings, looked for the three stars and lit candles, and discovered Sadie is Hebrew for Princess, nothing to do with Mexican cleaning ladies called Mercedes, which I'd always assumed was what Bob was thinking of. Was he calling her Sadie, too, the woman who obviously hadn't read Elmore Leonard and Carl Hiassen?

The carers rarely saw each other, but on the roster there were names like Vesna and Dragana, who'd have learnt things too while helping old ladies in and out of bathtubs, and patting them dry. What it was like being interned in Malaya, or running coffee plantations, which bridesmaid had given them the little crystal vase or the pansy-rimmed plate. Often there'd be something they had no further use for, a nice iron griddle, or a brass incense burner brought back by a seafaring husband, which carers weren't supposed to accept. Was that how it had been with Isobel and the old man in Inverness, whose watch they'd said she stole?

And sometimes it'd be things their children would give their right arms to know, or maybe not. Which one she could never bring herself to love as much as she'd loved the one who died.

'That's her up there, just before she got the meningitis. I held her in my arms on the tram, all the way to Crown Street. I still pray for her, every night.'

The kid, who'd dropped out to be a pro skateboarder, stopped getting fired by foremen called Darryn and Wayne and lasted a whole year in a warehouse with more forgiving older men, so Steve and She Who Must Be Obeyed bought him a plane ticket. But on 8 August, after seven blissful months, there's a call from Logan Airport, he's arrived with insufficient funds so they're required by law to send him back to Frankfurt, his point of embarkation, and you have a nice day, ma'am.

Tisha B'Av, the worst day in the Jewish year, I should have known [50]

***

It's an ill wind that blows no good, and as the recession wore on there was an investment property some poor woman had to sacrifice, the middle tranche of a three-storey terrace house in Surry Hills. This side of Oxford Street had seen more chance and necessity, lovely iron balconies bricked in after the war by my father's reffos, and others enhanced like mine with extensions and skylights and an atrium where my nodding violet cuttings, from the chirpy Bulgarian four doors down, soon tumbled down from my kitchen window box.

The cat had already lucked in by being dumped over Ita Buttrose's fence, as happens when you're President of the Cat Protection Society, and there he'd been in her office, a beautiful silver tabby sitting regally on a reproduction Louis Quinze chair. Please, please, she begs, it's like a maternity ward in here, we'll never get the next issue out.

So that was another ill wind. If I could have afforded to go into normal bookstores, I'd never have found that two-dollar remaindered copy of *How to Toilet Train your Cat in Three Weeks*. Three months more like it, with boys leaving the seat up or the lid down. For a while I'd thought of becoming a cat whisperer, making the world a better place by saving a gazillion trees and helping people avoid slipped discs schlepping supersize bags of litter. But terminally addicted as they now were to euphemism, they'd either misunderstand, or look dubious and go *yuk* at the thought of catching something. And by 2000 it's Robert de Niro in *Meet the Parents,* playing a retired CIA man, so they assume the only way is cruel and unusual punishments.

Beverley, who'd been a copy girl at *Woman's Day,* was rebirthing the house next door which had been a refuge for runaway kids. There went another career I'd envisaged, while getting rid of the mission brown bench-tops. Keep everything neutral, she says, *tabula rasa*, so buyers can imagine themselves expressing their creativity. I'd have thought it'd be more like *When Harry Met Sally,* I'll have what's she's having. The couple next door didn't even *have* a kitchen, just a sink, bar fridge and a microwave, and how long would that take to reach critical mass, as with the potato-washing monkeys? Or resonate morphically, as with the blue-tits able to open milk bottles?

The barrister who bought it gave a house-warming, wait-persons circulating with seaweedy nibbles and Schubert drifting out from the string quartet to the sandstone terrace where greenery already flourished in cobalt and celadon-glazed pots. I'd have soaked lemons overnight in a jar of rainwater, and sprinkled the whole place to pacify lingering spirits, not that *feng shui* worked at my place, or only horizontally, as downstairs was soon rented to two muscular blonde women who said they worked in a bridal shop and most nights there'd be uproar and destruction.

'Owners shoudda known,' said Bob. 'Sewing sequins don't pay the rent around here.'

So Tolstoy was right about that, if everyone killed their own animals, there'd be more vegetarians, only as usual they hadn't grasped the basic principle. And upstairs it was the IT girl and the composer who wouldn't commit. It was bad enough when I moved in, several Polynesians struggling to get my piano up two flights of stairs and negotiating the landing, but now it was every three months I'd be in the back bedroom with a pillow over my head, thinking Freud could have been right too. Those sweltering days when the car broke down and my father struggled to restart the engine, turning the crank handle again and again while my mother sits there with that pained expression and me with fingers crossed and my heart breaking again and again because I'm seeing him in a moment of weakness.

A little girl wants her father to be perfect, too big to fail, as they're saying these days.

***

The kid was now a bicycle courier, but there were always leftover pizzas or uneaten dinners, so I'd try doing the right thing by other people living in the community. There was still a Greek church, and a cake shop, but in Agi Kirikos there hadn't been old men sitting in shop doorways, like the one with the swollen red ankles, clutching a bottle, and a few paces down the one who stood eternally vigilant beside a red white and blue laundry bag, gazing across Taylor Square as his ancestors had once surveyed treeless Mongolian plains. It was easier to leave stuff beside the Chinese Presbyterians' yellow clothing bin. As Maimonides said, a gift where the giver is unknown to the recipient rates higher.

But one thing the old rabbis agreed on, you shouldn't hang around deserted places, the only person who'd ever got away with being remotely reclusive was J D Salinger, and only after he was famous. As if you have to be Jewish to be born with spectacles on your nose and autumn in your heart! And where would English literature be if people hadn't roamed moors and thought gentle melancholic thoughts in graveyards, whether there was an influenza epidemic that year, and why people stopped calling little girls Euphemia and switched to Lily and Violet. But I suppose even at my age you'd have to be helping people get married.

Even Michael had expectations, he'd moved on from 'now that'd be a nice job for you,' (an insomniac, he sometimes phoned in to a Mystic Majella about his share portfolio) and started talking implants, I'd be sure to meet a nice man. After Karl and Fiona's twin boys, there seemed little prospect of an Audacia, so I'd taken to pretending there'd been one already, though even dear old Mina never said any woman in our family had shot a bushranger, if anyone needed a shotgun pointed at him it was Uncle Wilfred/my grandfather. At least *her* father could control himself.

'Poor little thing, packed off to Glen Innes to stay with those awful people.'

But there'd definitely been no bushrangers in Johannesburg or Latvia, it was a win:win situation, me with the top left incisors taken care of and Michael going home to St Ives convinced he'd heard true tales of a pioneering past, a vanishing species like the Boers back home.

***

Being an ex-Marine, Bob had no trouble becoming a security guard, it was great meeting him for lunch, sidling up like Mae West and saying is that a gun in your pocket or are you just pleased to see me? Tuesday nights he had target practice and we'd go to the pistol range in the tunnel where the trams once rattled up from Wynyard. The hairdresser I'd had in my management days had gone there too, she said as a Libra she needed balance, a break from girly stuff, and it was what I needed too, after houses smelling of urine-sodden mattress and rotting bananas. Cordite and the creak of black leather jackets, the scent of male sweat when someone stood behind you, his big hands gently guiding your little ones.

Afterwards in The Hero of Waterloo we'd hear about four-wheel drives, the breeding habits of kangaroos and feral pigs, and GPS systems. Not that you can't sometimes be in two places at once, like after I'd interviewed Warren Mitchell and got two free tickets to see him playing Alf Garnett.

'Oh, that's going a bit far,' my mother keeps whispering, when I know it's the same only different from the last time we sat together in a dark place watching men going too far, that on the inside she's laughing now the way she was crying back then, at the army concert in 1943.

***

Poor old Aggie just wanted to die, if not now, then after the next episode of *The Bold and the Beautiful*, and another cigarette. Her kids had converted the garage into a granny flat, but if you didn't watch her there'd be another burn mark on the floral plastic tablecloth, her pink nightie, or some withered bit of herself. The only respite was when the physiotherapist came, a brightly smiling woman of a certain age who made Aggie walk around the garden with a Zimmer frame, and always spoke in the second person plural.

'We can't have our muscles atrophying, can we now?!'

Flashing a conspiratorial smile at me sitting under the tree, studying my Hebrew and wishing I could fire a few rounds into her, and all the others who saw nothing wrong in this charade. Or maybe did, but were too afraid to say so.

'Oh good girl, we'll have you running in the Olympics in no time! A real Cathy Freeman!'

Aggie had a sorrowful blonde Jesus in the kitchen where I'd make her teabag tea and remember her three spoonfuls of sugar. But Judaism has very few petitionary prayers, it's better to tell God how wonderful he is, has been, and will continue to be.

Nedar ba-kodesh, nora t'hilot.

One of them must have worked wonders, because Aggie died pretty soon afterwards.

[49] In 1994 the old Central Synagogue burnt down as the result of an electrical fault. The present one has women upstairs/men downstairs.

[50] The ninth day of the month of Av in the Hebrew calendar, the date of the destruction of the First and Second Temples in Jerusalem and subsequent tragedies, notably the expulsion of the Jews from Spain in 1492.

Chapter 16
Good Again

Inspector Rex would have sensed it immediately, that smell peculiar to government buildings where people wait in quiet desperation under inoffensive paintings of gum trees selected by a committee. Me and Cousin Mary, verging on eighty, on the day of my compensation case. Our family don't do litigation, let alone make a habit of it. Last time it was Wal leaving the boys some nugatory sum - a thousand each? They said courts no longer crucified women, but they were getting in practice for Pauline Hanson and Helen Darville.

Had I not, during my marriage, constantly been out with *men?* (Lawyers still didn't understand journalism). On more than one occasion, collected at the front gate in a chauffeur-driven Rolls? *Res ipse loquitur*, as Jiri would have said, exactly the sort of woman who'd produce ungrateful and undeserving sons. But again Victor and I saw them off.

It was when I'd been at *Australian Business,* so I'd been thinking lawyers! Either at your feet or at your throat, whereas with Deirdre it's No Change, Mary says she's telling everyone I'm 'suing the church'. As if we don't all know her own mother, dear old Mina, would have sued Veterans' Affairs if there'd been class action, strangled those shamelessly smiling weather girls too, 'another lovely fine day!' when farmers were desperate for rain.

That's another thing nobody ever told me, never speak highly of the mother of any woman who dislikes her as much as you dislike yours.

Now that Mina had gone I'd never know when, or to whom, my mother succumbed in *her* moment of weakness, after the soldier died. The bridegroom for whom the fatted calf was prepared, who tarried and never showed. Had Uncle Wilfred/my grandfather made seigneurial demands on the Chinese gardeners, for asparagus and strawberries?

'It was after that she became so ill, and nearly died.'

It's Mary who tells me things now, how she'd known yonks ago about her mother being brought home, to the discombobulation of mine, when Uncle Wilfred/my grandfather deemed sufficient time had elapsed. But unlike Mina, 'Proper little princess, nose quite out of joint,' she leaves you to connect the dots.

Like we'd often go to Double Bay for lunch and a movie, even a Woody Allen if I could persuade her it wouldn't be too Jewish. I knew what she meant, it's all about propinquity and she'd spent twenty years as receptionist for the ophthalmic surgeon who'd left Hungary long enough ago to have mellowed. Her second husband was a meat-and-three-veg man, so we'd be adventurous about lunch too, though I'm thinking Japanese might be a big ask, with her brother Ian surviving the Burma railway and her first husband killed in New Guinea. But she adores sushi and sashimi, she'd gone out with a Ken (Kenichi? Kenji?) a few times, nice chap, good job in a bank, only half Japanese ... and then it's 'isn't the pink ginger lovely?'

So after that it was even sadder, knowing what she meant when she'd tell people she was a widow at the wrong time of life.

Cousin Harry was dead too, the one who used to come to Nick's restaurant and show the kid how to draw Felix and Krazy Kat, not that any of us in Sydney knew until Ollie went up for Mina's funeral, or what *his* Japanese was called. We hadn't an inkling he'd even been ill, but when it came to secrecy Harry had form, all those years in England when he never wrote and his mother fretted her heart out thinking he might be dead. By the time I got to London, he was art director on some trendy magazine, and came to dinner in Hammersmith wearing a multi-coloured hand-knitted jumper and natty braces. But after he came back, Mary invited Harry home to dinner too, several times and despite the second husband (inviting me as well would definitely have been going too far) so it's nice to imagine that while they were stacking the dishwasher – 'careful, he might hear you!' –the cousins discovered an unexpected bond.

What Deirdre doesn't know, and mightn't have appreciated hearing as the ex-wife of an architect, is that the compensation case is because of another architect, or rather a house sacred to his memory with a dining-room table seating twelve, and umpteen cedar doors his widow wants to be able to see her face in, like it's the 1930s when she really did have Sadie the cleaning lady. Yet all I'd ever hear was 'but she's a dear old soul, show some compassion, it must be all that typing you used to do'. To the admin ladies, all the clients were dear old souls, it didn't take second sight to know they were thinking any minute it could be poor dear Mummy, how careful we'd have to be it wasn't some ghastly person! Even the carpal tunnel operation didn't help. Perhaps I needed another one?

Someone in the courtroom must have watched journalists at work, and realised it's not the same as data entry, because by lunchtime they'd awarded me a sum beyond my wildest imaginings. But by now I'm doing guilt pretty well myself, hearing not just the still small voice of conscience, but Rabbi Hillel's as well, regarding Phase Two of my education.

If not now, when?

They were right about use it or lose it – after five years, I was no more up for invading a mosque than scaling the north face of the Eiger. But tomorrow I could be knocked down by a bus, catch some virus or, God forbid, left totally paralysed and then I'd feel worse. So it was great that within weeks I could confidently answer 'Fifth of October', as Matt Dickie, a rug importer, had succumbed to the pleas of his clients and was about to lead his second tour.

I lost count of how many books they thrust upon me, with a chadored girl on the cover and straplines about persecution, rape and torture. Did Rabbi Hillel say anything about where? I don't think so.

**

One day in 1989, giving the health professionals the benefit of the doubt, I'd taken the kid to the German Expressionists at the Art Gallery. The only things that engaged his attention were George Grosz sketches, live black men playing saxophones or dead ones swinging on the end of a rope, but I'd bought a Karl Schmidt-Rottluff poster, circa 1920, of the older woman in the yellow dress looking nonjudgmental, and the wide-eyed daughter with the plaits who anyone can see won't think twice, another few years she'll be Heil Hitlering with the rest of them.

And now there they are in the flesh, what little of it isn't covered by black chadors, looming ahead as we wait in the women's line for customs and immigration, the older one almost benign and the young one itching for the good old days when she could remove your lipstick with a kerosene-soaked rag.

'The young are always the worst. Remember that Mitford girl who was mad for Hitler?'

Just about everyone on the tour was over sixty, rug tragics or retirees with limitless superannuation – after Patagonia and Kamchatka, where's left to go? Of course they remembered Unity, Diana who'd been mad for Moseley and Jessica mad about a Commie, maybe they'd even had daughters who'd once been mad for someone like the kid and already thinking there's much to be said for locking up girls.

Often Iranian women wouldn't get in the hotel lift with us, our only interaction had been with Fatima who'd invited us to share her ghalyan, which we did, though there were secret police everywhere – Western women behave shamelessly in teagarden! So in the Isphahan bank I wished the women's line had been twice as long, after the one ahead of me turned around and smiled.

Her husband had been killed in the Iran-Iraq war, but she and the two kids were sticking it out with his parents, really sweet folk, because look, it's just a passing phase. Yeah, sure she misses all kinda stuff, peanut butter, popcorn, movies, but don't talk to her about *Not Without My Daughter*, if she ever sees Sally Field she'll strangle her, that goddam lying bitch. [51]

Just as I was about to share similar feelings regarding Jane Fonda.

I'd already had one significant encounter with foreigners that day, striding off before breakfast from the Shah Abbasi Hotel past the furniture shops filled with P J O'Rourke's amazingly awful armchairs, to find what turns out to be a shabby corrugated iron gate guarded by two women with amazingly awful teeth. Am I imagining all those men inside with myrtle and willow? No, it's Sukkoth and my only mistake is arriving too early, as the women's session isn't until ten when we're due at the Armenians' Vank Cathedral.

At the Esteghlal in Tehran, the former Hilton, little had changed since 1979, gold and mission-brown decor, menus noting 'all salads served with Thousand Island dressing,' and chateaubriand steaks lost in translation, though not as badly as the *veau paupiettes,* which had turned into 'veal puppies.' But in Shiraz the huge gold signage in the foyer *Death to America! The Great Satan*, means exactly what it says, not nice when you're drinking non-alcoholic beer and have just come from places where they don't stop to ask, shouting and pounding the van until Matt, who speaks fluent Farsi, calms them down.

In Isphahan's Imam Mosque we stood exactly under the central dome, clapped once and heard seven echoes, one for each heavenly sphere. But we'd had a young local guide, Muzaffar, for the shaking minaret. It was more like a jumping castle, with four little turrets where you crawled in, jumped around, and were supposed to emerge awestruck.

'Yes, the earth moved for me, definitely. Was it good for you too?' Muzaffar wondering why all these women old enough to be his mother, with their sensible shoes and questions, their Omar Khayams and Xenophon's Persian Wars, are falling about giggling while the men smirk. What does Muzaffar know of Hemingway, the book or the movie, or of popcorn or coke? Definitely kinder to lie, keeping on telling him 'you done good' and teaching him useful phrases like 'a few prawns short of a barbie', appear confident things will change.

I don't think Nasr was lying though, at the computer shop in Redfern, the day I came in with the box of gaz, Isphahan's famous pistachio toffee.

'I was about ten and one day the Americans drove out in a big truck and put in all these struts and bolts.'

So had Muzaffar had known all along? I still think it was the decent thing to do, when someone needs all the hope he can get.

Back in Sultanahmet I bequeathed the loathsome *manteau* and the headscarves to the room attendant, revisited the Blue Mosque and explored the bookstores. They were full of books about the late Princess Diana and in the poorer suburbs the pavement stalls even had little shrines, like the ones for martyrs in Tehran. Today they'll tell you 1997 was the watershed moment in the crying game, but I still think it was the 1980s, the Lindy Chamberlain days, when more ceased to be less and too much could never be enough. It had just grown more sinister, no longer the expectation that major players should show emotion, but that onlookers, if they know what's good for them, should show it too.

*****

My story ran in *The Weekend Australian* in January 1998 and by May I'd scored a freebie, walking the pilgrim trail. Not the whole way, like the muscular German Christians and the fraught French (it was the new cure for mid-life crises), and only every second day, set down where we'd left off with a packed gourmet lunch and returned to a converted Basque farmhouse with *tout confort.*

When I'd lived in England it was maddening enough, asking what a red tree was and being told 'oh, I should think it's a copper beech.' But now every yellow flower was a buttercup. And why, in Basque churches, was it men who sat upstairs? The morning I was summoned by bells and raced across the valley past the placid creamy cows, there was no-one there – Dave, our tour leader, said most farmers had day jobs. But when we'd walk past those silent farmhouses with red peppers hung outside to dry, I'd imagine a grandmother inside, stringing more, tending newborn calves or puppies and preparing enormous daubes, and think wouldn't that be nice.

It wasn't until I got home, back to the Internet which I'd mastered with some help from the kid's latest girlfriend, Flora the dim-sim entrepreneur, that some Basque feminists in Nevada emailed that when churches were built over sacred sites, women were allowed to stay downstairs to tend their ancestors' graves.

It would have been something to tell Ollie, now he'd started raving about how religion only causes wars, no better than the rest of them. Some Aquarian he is! And it's anything but humane, verging on malicious, the way he'll sprinkle turmeric over my yoghurt and then say 'Oh, I'm so sorry, I forgot. You know it's so good for your prostate?'

***

Anywhere south of the Carpathians, *Lonely Planet* made it sound like a woman needed more than a wedding ring and photographs of grandchildren. Capsicum spray, at least, or a stiletto in her garter. But *The Australian* hadn't had a story on Romania for ages, and it'd help pay the plane fare.

Capitalism was thriving, hot-dog stalls on street corners where men in designer sunglasses indulged huge dogs called Attila and Vlad. Girls not yet fat teetered in clunky sandals, cradling tiny puppies, Mormons arrived *en masse* at Otopeni airport, and at quite a few railway stations leather-jacketed men would carry me off in their brother's or cousin's car, with bald tyres and a cracked windscreen, to their sisters' homestays.

What all Romanians remember is what they were doing the day Ceauşescu fell, 22 December 1989, starting with Victor, the geophysicist I'd found on the Internet, who told me over lunch (carp and mamiglia, but a nice Cotnari white) how in Piaţa Universităţii people clung cheering from every lamp post. I didn't have to imagine long, within days Romania beat England in the World Cup. So I shared my memories, part of them anyway, about why I'd never forget what I was doing when Ceauşescu had just ascended, the night in Adelaide when I'd knocked on Irving's door. He'd been reading *Time Magazine*, and I'd lain down beside him, heart pounding at my audacity, and read it too, the cover story about Ceauşescu being the West's new best friend [52]

In Sighisoara it's positively Shakespearian, Petronella's mother hauling up her jumper in the middle of dishing out pigs' testicle soup to show me her hysterectomy scars, these wounds I had in the Ceauşescus' day, while aunts and sisters recall illegal unanaethetised abortions. I forget how many (in the attic Jiri's girlfriend had only seen the man from the Underground doing

193

one, to someone with her mouth stuffed with rags) because Petronella's father is plying me with his homemade *tuica,* and fondling my red toenails.

How could I object, with nothing to declare but my contact lenses and the near-invisible scars on my eyelids? Besides, a guest shouldn't criticise her host's concept of personal space when it's obvious there wouldn't *be* any guests if the family weren't all sleeping in the living room.

That's another thing I'd always wondered, whether there's some geographical watershed – like north of the Pyrenees, you don't get vultures – between places where nothing's too much trouble, and those where guests shouldn't create difficulties, if pig's testicle soup is all there is, tough. When I was a girl, everyone knew it was the English Channel, '(wogs begin at Calais'), then I thought it must be the Alps, and later, somewhere above Greece. Now it's just another thing nobody notices.

The way Petronella and her sisters rummaged through my suitcase in search of peanut butter, they were obviously accustomed to Americans, but in the middle of watching *Annie Hall,* it's 'Woody Allen's *Jewish?*' Like it's news to them any made it across the Atlantic, perhaps that there's any left at all. Yet every family had a photograph on a little lace doily of some relative, the graduate who'd made it to the States or Canada, the way every stall in Iranian bazaars had a photograph of the family martyr in paradise. Perhaps lucky Romanians sent tapes like my mother used to send to me in London, only mentioning huge buildings, freeways and amazing progress, however many flavours of ice-cream there were by 1997.

***

Driving from one old lady to another, I'd listened more often to 2MBS-FM, and had volunteered, imagining it'd be blissful, a couple of days a week listening to the classics while checking the umlauts in *Götterdämmerung.* But I'm barely in the door before it's the same old, sent off to schmooze total strangers while the retired newspaper men get to discuss Bach and swap rude jokes.

Riley Lee tells me over lunch he spent years learning the *shakuhachi* on Sado Island, but it has a long tradition of sadness because it's where the Japanese once sent social deviants to work the silver mines, so perhaps not. I'd just have to remember Father Merritt in the charcoal burners' hut, in the forest where there'd once been bears

***

After Iran, I wanted to maintain momentum, but how? There were now two mosques in Surry Hills, but the little one in Cleveland Street was Turkish men only and the big one in Commonwealth Street had a daunting iron-barred fence. Rabbi Hillel must have reached the end of his patience, because one day I slipped up. Everyone's amazed, assuring me they've never have suspected, but even so, attention must be paid.

'It's probably another election year.'

'Think positive! You owe it to yourself!'

And early in December, around midnight on a windy corner of Taylor Square, I break my rule about never buying *The Sydney Morning Herald,* and this time my name is there. I'm about to become an educated woman.

***

In liberal Jewish circles one thing which got you *yichus,* respect, was having a Bernays in your family – in the 1820s, Rabbi Isaac Bernays in Hamburg had been a hero of the *Haskalah,* the first to preach in German instead of Hebrew. So that summer I trawled through the phone directory, and next thing it's me being enlightened over dinner in Woolstonecraft with Gay, née Bernays, who has the complete family tree. The one I'd have noticed thirty years ago at the Freud Museum if I'd felt less miserable, and could have asked Clement Freud about over dinner a few year later if we hadn't been having too much fun.

When Max had told me about Napoleon making Jews get proper surnames, my impression had been they didn't have much choice, but maybe it was like Irish lawyers, as in Mainz two brothers were allowed to adapt the name of their father, Jacob Baer of Neustadl. Isaac the fruit merchant converted but Jacob the innkeeper didn't, and it was the fourth of Jacob's eight children who became the famous rabbi. But the rabbi too had an apostate brother, Adolphus who went to England to become professor of German language and literature at Kings College, and ultimately the grandfather of my great-uncle Charlie. While back in Germany the rabbi's second son, Berman, had a daughter Martha who became Mrs Sigmund Freud – and a son Eli who married Freud's sister Anna, of whose son Edward Bernays, the father of public relations, the less said the better.

I ran all this past Ollie when I went down to Melbourne in January, sitting in his back garden under the Chinese gooseberry tree which unlike the ones in Northern Portugal manages only a few feeble fruit. Our family thought *that* was bad, poor Annie marrying below her station, at least he was C of E. And what of the rabbis's son Michael who converted and never married at all? Do you think his mother was like Mina was about you, always hoping he'd find a nice girl? If only Charlie and Effie had had kids, the brilliant cousins we could have married!

But it was no use, heredity only sets him off about brown-eyed people, as they mostly are in his neighborhood. I even had a word with his old orchestra mates, but propinquity *vincit omnia*. 'His bark's worse than his bite', they said, 'and wasn't his mother a lovely old soul?' Even so, on the nights I'd make prawn or chicken stir-fry (Ollie was now convinced red meat gives you cancer), I'd walk to the shops myself to be on the safe side. And the only time he mentioned Mina, it was how she'd dragged them to church every Sunday, how one year they all saved up to buy her a riding crop for her birthday, and the first thing she did was wallop him with it.

***

[51] *Not Without My Daughter*, 1991, American citizen Betty Mahmoody/Sally Field and her daughter escape from her brutal Iranian husband and ultra-religious family.

[52] *Time Magazine,* 18 March, 1966, had Ceaușescu on the cover, with a strapline, *'Life Under a Relaxed Communism'*.

Chapter 17
Millennium Days

'Apart from the assassination, Mrs Lincoln, how did you enjoy the play?' -Old journalists' joke.

***

There had to be a catch somewhere.

'What if I get Alzheimer's?' I'm holding up the queue, a couple of hundred school leavers, on enrolment day.

'You look far too young.' They're no longer allowed to say you look far too old.

'You realise I'll never be able to repay the HECS?' They also can't say 'who'll give an old bat like you a job, even with a dozen degrees?'

'Not a problem'. He's been doing his PhD for seven years now, it'll be another seven if ever before he's earning enough. So I too think long term.

'They won't try clawing it back after I'm dead? I've got five grandchildren to think about.'

'No way. Just sign here.'

I'd always wondered what it meant, to kick an own goal. Now I knew.

***

Thanks to the Internet I also now knew that when Marx wrote about the idiocy of rural life, he meant it the Greek sense, idiosyncratic, meaning country people still retained their individuality. Nor did he quite say history repeated itself, as tragedy and then as farce, he was saying Hegel *ought* to have said it, and they could both have been right – the first time I'd been younger than all the students, now I was older than all the lecturers. But wherever old Anglos came from, they were responsible for all the trouble in the world, and *wie es eigentlich gewesen* meant not what actually happened, but what ought to have happened if they'd been there at the time.

Islamic Studies, a tiny class of twenty or so, was mostly people who were idiosyncratic to start with, foxes who already who knew a heap of things and not always little ones. Tony, even older than me, who'd been torpedoed in the Persian Gulf during WW2 and drifted semi-conscious on a plank for days; boys who'd hitchhiked across Turkey; Rachel who loved belly-dancing, and Michelle whose second husband was an Iranian Bahia with a price on his head. She was doing law, to specialise in immigration, and had a crazy kid too, yet still found time to cook wonderful crusty *tah-dig* rice and cheese pastries for our class picnics under the jacaranda in the quad. There was even a boy in a pretty embroidered *yarmulke*, but not for long, and Ben who'd been a Buddhist for years. Later I heard the Bosnian with the butterfly tatt fell in love with him and it all ended badly.

There were girls in *hijab,* a few from Turkey looking gorgeous, and one or two from Afghanistan, but mostly from Marrickville and Lakemba, often quite ferocious. Had they too broken their parents' hearts, like the *baal teshuvahs?*

We learnt about Ibn Battuta, who travelled to places Marco Polo probably just pretended to, and the Nasser era, when it had stood to reason that once exposed to higher education, women throughout the Middle East would soon be like Hudá Sha'arāwī who'd famously removed her veil, to wild cheers, on Cairo railway station in 1923. But in the 1950s it was thousands of girls coming down from Aswan, or up from the Delta – the provinces – who hadn't just returned from a feminist conference in Europe, being confronted in Cairo by something the same as, only different from, the ice-maidens on the sandstone steps at St Lucia. Smoking, drinking, exposing their bosoms to the lewd glances of men.

I cheered a bit myself. At last, I was hearing my story!

But by 2008, it was *plus ca change.* Having abandoned all hope of finding a tour of Egypt that wouldn't be about Pharoahs and dead people, I went by myself, and slogged up and down Cairo's Talat Harb Street for hours asking *'wayna* Yacoubian Building?'[53] In 1934 the Armenian millionaire Hagop Yacoubian intended it to be a posh address, but by the 1990s Alaa-Al-Aswany has his first dentistry practice there and sees it as something quite different, a metaphor for Egyptian society. It was alongside a menswear store, and just as I'm admiring the Art Deco signage, silver on an aquamarine ground, (which for some reason is on the *inside*), in walks a *hijab*ed girl who lives on the famous roof! By now it was too dark to estimate how many other people were living up there in the old laundry sheds, but I drank hibiscus tea with her, in a sort of canvas lean-to, and heard about the problems girls from Aswan face at university.

But in 1999 *The Yacoubian Building* was four years in the future, and that wasn't the only unknown unknown. Rabia, the pharmacist with the lustrous black hair and crimson fingernails, didn't tell me for years that she was a Wahhabi. Beyond Islamic Studies few people had heard of them, or of Sunnis or Shi'as either, and outside university, they often assumed we were just learning Arabic.

And if anyone had known that the previous time Pluto was in perihelion, between 1730 and 1750, was when the Wahhabi were born in Arabia, and set about destroying Sufi shrines, it wouldn't have helped a bit. Gone were the days when the *Pickwick Papers* and *The Adventures of Tintin* could be safely continued in the next issue, which rarely took longer than a month.

With university, too, a lot depends on where *you've* been, what your *behaviours* will be, and I had plenty to choose from. For a start there was nothing like an integrated universe. The departments all lived in little boxes, any of this 'only connect' business and they'd be calling you a conspiracy theorist even if you weren't a Queenslander. Ten years on, post-Mohammad Hanif, they'd have been strip searching us for exploding mangoes.[54]

My first thought was Centrelink with lawns, and then that middle management required drastic pruning. Later, in Roman History, we heard it had taken fewer people to administer the Roman Empire at its peak. The lecturer was about to retire, so we also heard that once upon a time, half the class would have been able to read Theodor Mommsen's *Romischer Geschichte*. I'd also thought there'd have been something like a meet'n'greet, where students got to eyeball the lecturer before committing.

Yet academe had cottoned on to many features of the corporate world, including some long known to be useless, like exit questionnaires. I'd still be scribbling away long after everyone else had ticked yeah, yeah, terrific and gone for a beer, though sometimes the mature students (translation: people over twenty-five) went to campaign for an on-campus crèche.

Q: Has this course contributed to your understanding of teamwork?

A: We're not working in a Volvo factory!

Q: Helped you communicate more effectively? Enhanced your ability to plan your studies and organize your priorities?

A: Some of us have had a life!

That's lions for you. It's not just admiration, too much gratitude is never enough either

***

Islamic Studies allowed for a lot of connection, and huge

economies of scale. With the Medieval History essay, 'Did the Normans in Twelfth Century Sicily Create the First Multicultural State?' I was the first person who'd ever mentioned eunuchs. In the Muslim world eunuchs had great career options – treasurers, financial administrators or admirals – so when you included those doing the usual women's work, it's arguable the Normans faced the most powerful minority group in history, had eunuchs not been riven by the usual factional squabbles. Or would have been arguable, had there been the slightest primary evidence. That was definitely just me, checking out the only book there was, a French one on the various techniques for creating eunuchs, not all of which worked as intended, being effectively vasectomies.

Mythology One was an enormous class, ninety percent women, predominantly girls, and eighty percent of them wanted to write about Athena. As the essay topic was Olympian gods, Uranus wasn't an option, but I could have made a good case for Aphrodite, Botticelli's Venus arising from the foam after the severed testicles splashed into the sea – as the mother of conflict resolution. But whoever you chose, Artemis/Princess Diana ruled, they wanted a fifteen hundred word Homeric ode as well, all flowery effusions and grand sentiments.

Thanks to *Forum* I couldn't resist Early Modern Europe, which promised sex and violence. Religion was held responsible for most of it, we spent weeks on the Inquisition and the slave trade, though only between West Africa and North America. But at some stage European populations had fluctuated wildly due to erratic harvests, so I made what I thought was a useful observation.

Breastfeeding was a *contraceptive*? They couldn't have been more astonished if I'd hauled up my shirt to reveal supernumerary nipples, like the other Artemis at Ephesus. Here too it was mostly school leavers, quite a few Asians, but even the lecturer, who was gay, needed filling in about luteinizing hormones. But just as well I raised the subject, as afterwards he told us that until the mid-1940s, when historians heard about the effects of starvation on the menstrual cycles of women in concentration camps, they'd thought population declines were because people hadn't wanted to bring children into such a horrible uncertain world. A sure sign they'd grown up reading too much Ernest Hemingway, and if any of them were women, they'd never gone to boarding school.

***

From the 1960s onward, they were fond of quoting Robert Frost, *home is where, when you go there, they have to take you in.* Same principle as the Arabic *watan*, and quite unlike the French *patrie,* which is more about the concept of nation states which, given the lost-in-translation factor and the tendency of young men to get excited by the wrong bits, doesn't work too well when you transplant it to the Middle East.

As Professor Shboul kept saying, any country whose borders are mostly straight lines is born to trouble. But after the bad day when I'd said 'oh, so Arabic's like Hebrew?' regarding the three root consonants, I knew to avoid rabbinical behaviour, like asking what about Poland, nothing but trouble and never a straight line to be seen? Or whether Portugal and Spain could be sued retrospectively for the Treaty of Tordesillas of 1494, whereby Longitude 51W00 (give or take a few hundred leagues) and its antimeridian 129E00, the straightest of straight lines, was used to divide the known world between them, neither country dreaming that Australia was there, with something not unlike *watans*, and would itself need dividing one day.

***

In 1993, in Japan, the villagers of Inakadate planted their fields with different strains of rice to create various iconic art works, which you're unaware of until you're cruising at thirty-five thousand feet or so, looking down at Hokusai's great wave, samurai and manga heroes, and of course it didn't end there. The Mona Lisa you can understand, Che Guevara and Chairman Mao could be down there too. But Napoleon on his white horse?! As Japanese villagers could hardly be remembering pre-war Australian biscuit tins, maybe it said more about Japanese universities, that being in love with France was becoming endemic.

As well as the eunuch book, Fisher Library also had one explaining that France was where American postgraduate students yearned to go, ideally Paris (in the footsteps of their sainted Thomas Jefferson) but failing that any place with drinkable wine and decent schools for the kids, for instance the Languedoc which had once tolerated sensitive troubadors and Cathars who'd practised gender equality. But nothing beat the French Revolution, any old revolution anywhere – Dame Edna was right, it's the colour and movement they love – so the only English history course was not the Glorious Revolution of 1688, entirely bloodless, not a single decapitation with heads on pikes or used as footballs, but the Civil War, 1642-1651, which due to the collapse of censorship they also considered a golden age for journalism. The happy hours I spent, writing an essay on our sainted William Lilly!

My best discovery, after Dr John Ward's course on Dante (at last, *Paradiso*!) was his 'Manicheans, Bulgars and Vegetarians'. It was another tiny idiosyncratic class, but mostly women – a Goth who loved Buffy the Vampire Slayer, a pretty blonde who worked in a fairy shop, and another who sometimes turned up wearing a medieval embroidered corset. For a while it was heavy going, dualism and the nature of evil, but with the Babylonian exile and Canaanite myths I perked up, arguing that the concept of fallen angels could only mean the Book of Enoch had been written before anyone understood the phenomenon of retrogradation.

Possibly this was another of Pythagoras's triumphs, proving around 530 BC that the morning star and the evening star were not, respectively, bad guy and good guy, but the same planet, Venus, which on its conjunction with the sun becomes invisible for about fifty days before reappearing in the west. In other words, crime and punishment, hubris and nemesis, had nothing to do with it, it hadn't plummeted to earth as a fallen angel, or a meteorite which would ultimately become a focus for fertility rites, like the Ka'aba at Mecca.

***

If blame must be attributed, going to Yemen was all Professor Shboul's fault for making Arabia Felix sound so exciting. Venturesome Greeks thwarted by coral reefs, then Pliny's sailors swooning before it was even visible, overcome by breezes laden with the scent of cloves and cinnamon. *Mu'allaquat* poems about girls with waists as slender as a camel's nose rein, and tamarind trees uprooted by wild desert storms inundating the wadis. But Manfred Wenner's *Modern Yemen 1918-1966* was absolutely right, it was indeed hurtling headlong into the fourteenth century.

The tour I'd found on the Internet, imagining it'll be full of intrepid Europeans, turns out to be two Americans, Corey and Steve, sitting either side of me in the back of the Toyota 4WD, bouncing through a landscape where every scruffy shrub flies a different-coloured plastic bag, while Muhammad, our Shi'a guide and already the father of ten, explains, from the front seat, the difference between Islamic law and tribal law regarding men caught having unnatural sexual relations. Under one system they're castrated and dismembered before being hurled from a minaret and under the other it's the reverse.

It's probably one of Jung's insoluble mysteries, whether people do things deliberately or, as Jesus said, they simply don't realise. I've always favoured the first, giving them credit for some intelligence, and Muhammad had been doing it for days, even more so after we'd stopped at the new brick pharmacy in the middle of nowhere. It's locked but we can see through the window that apart from plastic nappies and L'Oreal hair dye it's mostly packets of prescription drugs from Syria or India (the Second World?) and a lot of one in particular, which either Steve or Corey, after a slight hesitation, tells me is um, some kinda muscle relaxant.

Qat or no *qat,* Muhammad didn't miss much. I'd be having a quiet smile myself at lunch (always huge because he needed a full stomach to get started) the way they'd go on about who'd been to Burkina Faso twice, or all of Oman and not just the north or the south.

The WHO, and many NGOs, classified *qat* as a drug and wanted to ban it – President Saleh's three wives had just quit, to set a good example. A few years later, in La Paz, I'll see a whole museum about how they don't understand coca either. For a start, *qat's* much easier to grow than coffee, any old woman or a little girl can be left in charge while her menfolk are off in Saudi Arabia. Far more crucial is its role in social bonding when they return with washing machines and televisions strapped on top of their spluttering sedans. If you don't sit around for hours smoking *qat* with them, the rest of the village will think you've got above yourself, looking down on them because their wives are still trampling their washing in the ravine.

Qat encourages eloquence and wild flights of fantasy, and by mid-afternoon Muhammad would be on about how it depresses the appetite, make *qat* into a pill and Yemen's economic problems would be solved overnight. He never mentioned it's also constipating and discourages erections, so I didn't ask how much of that stuff in the pharmacy was Viagra. [55]

When the *qat* wore off, Muhammad would revert to his normal surliness. In Yemen, unlike Iran, you could bring in whisky and one night, walking after dinner down some dusty street past eucalypts and wary dogs, I asked why there's no *Qu'rans* in the bedrooms.

'They might be touched by menstruating wimmens!'

And every day he'd come back scowling from some military checkpoint or petrol station where he'd met some Zaydi who wasn't the sort he was, or who'd fought for equally faction-ridden Peoples' Democratic Republic of Yemen. The unification, in May 1990, seemed hardly worth the trouble.

The worst day was up by the Saudi border, when the three of us are barely breathing – you don't want a man becoming more afraid of you than you are of him when he's holding a Kalashnikov. His mates have carried Muhammad off in a flatbed truck with a machine gun (which I know from Steve, ex-NASA, is capable of taking out a small aircraft) and we can see them on a small rise, about two hundred metres away, Muhammad a small white figure with arms extended helplessly, looking disturbingly like Jesus, so I almost feel sorry for him. But then he starts walking back and his body language tells us we'd better keep on keeping quiet until he's finished riffling through the stash of dollars in his briefcase.

Yet half an hour later at Al-Harf there he was at the cash desk chatting away like they're his new best friends. Probably paying for their lunch, and the petrol too.

The best day was when we set out around four in the morning, President Saleh in the Seventies mural with his Afro hair and kipper tie beaming down as we crossed the foyer of the Hotel Bilqis, aka Sheba, to find Venus splendidly risen above the oleanders. We go hurtling into the Hadramaut, scattering wild camels and charging over sand dunes, like George Clooney in *Three Kings*. The further east we went, the more Saddam Hussein smiled down at us in truckies' caffs – once unnervingly from beside a poster of Sydney Harbour – and the more starving Somali women stood outside, waiting for the busboy to bring them leftover bread and goat stew.

At a government rest house in Tarim I swam in an ancient pool ringed by more pink oleanders, imagining Freya Stark doing the same in the 1930s, while Corey and Steve, who'd never heard of her, played table tennis under a pepperina aka pilpul tree. And again in the Arabian Sea, at Mukalla where Hungarian and Polish scuba divers were revisiting the scenes of their youth. Maybe they too ate a divine goat curry somewhere, a sacrificial one for Eid al-Adha, and felt sorry for the people staying in the Holiday Inn, newly built by some wealthy family called bin Laden.

***

My Yemen story ran in May 2000, everything looked on track for my becoming a travel writer specialising in the Middle East. In Fisher some of the school leavers who'd checked out Gender and Patriarchy in first year could have been envisaging new careers too. They now checked out books on Peace Studies and Media Communications.

Still, in first year I'd been a bit clueless myself. Accustomed to public libraries, I'd thought only unemployed people and ageing pedants scribbled comments in books, even I had corrected faulty apostrophes and the occasional transposed lines. The marginalia in Islamic Studies books had therefore been a revelation, all outrage and passionate intensity – Lying Zionist pig! This Jewish infidel insults Allah! Sometimes whole sentences blacked out. It didn't look like the Gender Studies girls, our chief competitors.

But by 2000 there'd definitely been an escalation, more of it in Arabic, too, written with such ferocity that sometimes the page would be torn. Surely it couldn't be any of us either.

Not when they've been telling the world for years that only the poor, uneducated, superstitious Muslims felt that way – the van-rockers in Iran and the Yemeni men sitting on a bench at Bayt al-Faqih market with a row of goats' horns cupped to their spines. As if the educated ones, who'd realised how much the West could offer them, would ever dream of doing anything terrible.

***

One thing anyone can predict is that their second class reunion won't be as good as the first, but how could I have foreseen, or Denny Lawton either when she'd set the date for 15 September 2001, that it'd be just me who hadn't had a child or a grandchild at work in one or other tower, or a husband's second cousin who'd normally have been there, but miraculously wasn't?

You'd have thought someone would have been up for discussing God moving in a mysterious way, or just the workings of fate which had already put a kibosh on things, with both my older boys having mid-life crises. Nick had done a runner, (*Sell Park Lane*) otherwise being executive chef at luxury tropical resort would have rated high, and Karl was about to be fired by the owner of the new gym he was managing. The kid, as usual, would've been *Go Directly to Jail*. He did once, just overnight, but 2001 was when he'd had to go grape-picking in Victoria before somebody called Stuart, who claimed he was owed $10,000, could break both his legs.

***

[53] Alaa-Al-Aswani, *The Yacoubian Building*, American University in Cairo Press, 2003, best-selling Arabic novel translated into twenty-three languages and filmed in 2006.

[45] Mohammed Hanif, *A Case of Exploding Mangoes*, Knopf/US 2008, comic

novel about the plane crash that killed former President of Pakistan, Muhammad Zia ul-Haq.

[55] Yemen's Ministry of Health allowed Viagra imports in 1998, by 2000 each pharmacy sold, on average, thirty to forty capsules a month.

Chapter 18
Roots Revisited

By May 2003 there's documentary evidence I've been saved and rescued, the cap-and-gowned woman, flanked by two towering men, who's known for some time why they're getting taller every time she kisses them, it's not just her high heels sinking into the soggy lawn. But even pre-Photoshop an image didn't always show the truth. For I am not *redeemed* at all, quite the opposite, only they still hadn't got it, despite the millennium which hadn't been about the saved being swept rapturously up, but the doomed plunging horribly down.

Anything but admit a systemic failure!

Eumundi was over what I now knew is called traditional*ism*, which unlike Edward Said's *Orientalism* can be self-imposed in the cause of tourism. But in November 2002, six weeks before I relocated, Cousin Mary phoned to say my stepbrother Ian had died. In October he'd told me the new pacemaker would be probably be right in a cuppla days, but better I didn't call by just now.

So now I'd never know where my pony's grave was, and which farm it was on Mineshaft Road where we'd picked the beans, just down the road from the little pole house waiting for me in the woods. The vendor who lived across the gully had built it for her mother, so it could have been waiting from the minute she'd died, confident its destiny was to go on being loved for its cathedral ceilings, the stained-glass Art Nouveau window, and the kitchen that's exactly right.

Soon every second person is telling me they went to Ian's funeral, and how he'd asked to be buried in his old work boots and khaki shorts, the ones he'd been wearing the last time I ever saw him, when Jenny and I drove up to recover from the crinolined women at the spinning wheels, and drank tea in the old breakfast room where the flip charts of planes once hung over the yellow pebble glass door. How small it now seemed, though you expect that. Never that he'd suddenly get up and come back with a photograph, 'you might like to have this, Jamtin'. Just a distant shot of her, in a longish white WW1 dress, standing on the veranda of the house that burnt down, but the first one I'd ever seen.

And was that also meant to be, that instead of staying on to be asked questions he mightn't have wanted to answer, *wie es eigentlich gewesen* regarding Kathleen, he'd left it to others to tell me what's more important?

Mona Seib, who used to pull my plaits at school, had gone to his funeral too, and isn't the only one who remembers Ian always stopping for a yarn if you met him on the road on his old brown horse, with the two cattle-dogs. And she too said it was as if he'd known beforehand and was up there laughing in the Tewantin funeral parlour, not because they'd got his name wrong but because it's all happening around three on the first Tuesday in November.

Mona owns the dairy that I walk to every second morning, leaving the money in the tin in the cool-room. But if I wake in the night and need milk for a coffee, I can drive down because she's shown me where they hide the key.

There were five white McMansions now at the end of the ridge where our sharefarmer's cow bails used to be, and around Mt Cooroy the hills were alive with white alpacas belonging to a retired Sydney lawyer. 'You know Ian saved my life a couple of years back? I was pinned under the tractor and he went and got a chain saw'. He runs upstairs to find his wife's red alpaca evening

212

dress, light as a feather, while I admire his lily pool and a painting by some indigenous artist of the Pleiades. Who would have thought it, that a myth would escape explosion? Though they predicted it themselves, the way they used to say half an hour after you've eaten a Chinese meal you need another one.

I considered my field, cleared the little dam where the wild melons grew, dredged the two long-silted watercourses, along which I planted twenty trees, black bean, red cedar and silky oak, and extended the orchard with mango and persimmon trees.

My family expanded too – firstly with Nichola's boyfriend, whose stepfather had told him that his biological father was a Basque terrorist; and then, by one degree of separation, a charismatic dictator. Not a military man, but as an educated woman I can tell you the minute any country starts letting men go to Paris, next thing it's a coup or a revolution. By February 2003 scarlet bougainvillea was frothing around the brass plates of the Cuban and Libyan Embassies, and though he'd done dictating they were still electing him, accustomed to his face which still smiled down in every public building, clean-shaven with silver sideburns. I could see why her mother fell for him.

In the supermarket it was still no butter one week and no bacon the next, and a black market in bath plugs, but it's better to agree he did much for the environment, eradicating feral goats and saving several rare species of tortoise. Otherwise my small brown about-to-be daughter-in-law mightn't take me to see Ferdinand, the *gris-gris* man who lives in the canefields and is visited by angels.

Elle veut savoir si elle va jamais rencontrer un homme gentil, she says, or a Creole approximation. But he just smiles and says I'll probably be too busy, which isn't too disheartening. As Chandler said, a good detective never gets married.

Two weeks later, twenty kilometres out of Salta, Argentina,

the *bruja* next door has an asphalt car park and accepts credit cards, but investigation is out of the question as every morning there's freshly munched and trampled stalks in our cornfield because according to Irene, who's gone back to her ex-husband's roots, she's undoing the fence every night and sending in her cows. I'm thinking that's easily solved, Irene should try tying her dog up at night so it won't chase the witch's sheep. But detectives don't have to deal with magical realism, a tiny black velvet bag tucked in the brickwork bordering the vegetable patch, stuffed with hair and stitched with red thread. The same red thread, says Irene, that the *bruja* uses to stitch up a toad's mouth after she's stuffed in a piece of the knickers belonging to whichever woman her client is hopelessly in love with.

It was good to come home and solve more ordinary mysteries.

***

With the nursery rhyme there were people from Alaska to Zanzibar, all with some Scandinavian connection, who remembered fragments, or even saw a political subtext, but everyone agrees the first line is, or a variant of, *Ride ride ranke*/ride 'em cowboy, even when the second line doesn't mention a *Rappschecke,* the German word for a piebald. Glenny the horse-whisperer was dead, but her little sister Betty had written a book on pioneer families, discovering so many Danes had lived out past Kenilworth there was actually a place called Little Denmark.[56] The grand seigneur was a retired photographer called Poul Poulsen, who'd had several younger brothers back in Schleswig-Holstein, then German, and when each one became old enough for military conscription, he'd be off to Australia to join the family business, which endured for a hundred years.[57]

So picture this, a hundred years of female Poulsens, aged

anywhere from eight to eighty, bouncing a fretful tot on their knees, probably several in succession, while a photographer fiddled under a black cloth and told Grannie and Aunt Effie, Uncle Wilfred/my grandfather's four straw-boatered sisters, and Aunt Trudie and my mother in ringlets and long white muslin dresses, to stay still and say cheese. (The Danish word *ost* would never have worked). Indulging the child by making the horse the same colour as its own, bay or brown, white or chestnut. As there were Poulsen studios all over southeast Queensland, there must be thousands of us.

By 1907, David George Verrier from South Africa was already a man of mystery, only coming into town to sell his timber, yet never missing a school picnic, where the children taunted him with rude names. Obviously he forgave them, because in 1927 he donated land for a tennis court and a hall provided it was never used for dancing or the consumption of liquor. But what nobody expected, (said Hessie Lindsell the local historian) was that he'd had a wife and children, who'd either died or decamped. So whether he was a buggy-whip-wielding authoritarian or a raging drunk, who'd either way repented, I'll keep on seeing Mr Verrier as I always imagined him, a foreigner with a tragic past, and braver than I ever was, to have stood and watched other people's happy children at play.

But with Chandra Lal, I'd been way off. The Queensland government, thinking banana-growing would be nice for returned WW1 soldiers to settle down to, had brought about twenty Indians from Fiji, single men who began as farm labourers, cutting weeds with a nifty flail nobody had seen the like of. But they'd soon acquired land and cows, which they understood much better than bananas, and all seem to have married local girls – in Nambour Library I found a death notice for one who'd had about ten kids. But even assuming the others did too, it wouldn't necessarily follow that the Sunshine Coast is now full of people who know how to make a proper curry.

***

There were five donkeys on agistment, with the usual twee Victorian names, keeping my grass down. If you stood on the deck making honking noises, within seconds they'd come trotting up to the electric fence, gazing up hopefully in expectation of carrots or bits of pumpkin. Euphemia and Dolly were the worst, and if Felix, Ignatius and Polly thought I was coming down to sort it out they were much mistaken, I'd better things to do, teaching myself Italian and figuring out where Orion's Belt would be by ten o'clock, over the mulberry tree or more towards the camphor laurels - which some of them now called *weeds,* already forgetting some people were once called vermin.

Over my dead body anyone gets rid of mine, I'd think, or the impatiens or the African tulip tree either.

Of course if the donkeys had belonged to me I might have felt differently, like I did about Freud now he was part of the family. A man who loved cats can't have been all bad - time spent watching them is never wasted, he said. But how different the world might be if he'd watched donkeys as well.

The Italian, apart from wanting to read Guiseppe de Lampedusa, was because I'd planned to look at Florence before going to a conference in Cambridge in September 2003 on Jewish and Muslim influences on Dante. But in March the Americans had invaded Iraq again, and while it was pretty foreseeable that old fault lines would re-open there, they opened even sooner in England, speakers refusing to be seen dead on the same platform as some other speaker, so the conference never happened and I went to Morocco instead. Somewhat sulkily, being convinced there'd be nothing to write because everyone except me was there in the Sixties getting stoned, so their children would've gone too, to see where their parents were once young and foolish.

Even on a tiny acreage invasion is part of life, if it wasn't flying foxes attacking the grapefruit it'd be the three guinea-hens, nervous and none-too-bright creatures whose chief value, while alive, is as an early warning system, like the cackling geese who saved Rome from the Gauls in 390 BC – though with foxes, alpacas do it better. They came from across Kenilworth Road, where the gravel trucks thundered, and I was sorely tempted when I found one still warm and barely grazed. But I plucked some speckled feathers and put them in the crazed Persian vase, not that Max had ever specifically mentioned road-kill being *treyf,* but because I'd thought of him back when there'd still been three guinea-hens. The day he started singing, softly in a beautifully modulated voice, over the Szechwan prawns

'Oh dear, what can the matter be? Three old ladies locked in the lavatory.'

So he probably sang it to every new girlfriend, what's it matter, and no point either telling Ollie now he's got a hearing aid and leaps like a startled deer whenever I say something, telling me there's no need to shout, and to enunciate my consonants more clearly, so when I do he can look even more aggrieved and say 'there's no need to sound like an Italian'.

And whenever I'd urge him to read de Tocqueville's *Democracy in America,* fair's fair, after all I read his Christopher Hitchens, bagging Mother Teresa, he'd just put on his video of Beethoven's Fourth, the start of the second movement, with Mitsuko Uchida (never mind *her* brown eyes) at the piano, in her filmy sea-green dress, and say 'Listen! The soft gentle voice of reason, hear how she gradually commands attention, triumphs over the baying of the mob*!'*

Well, true. But I'm thinking more of Pat Rolfe at the *Bulletin* smiling her stealthy smile, sending me off to interview yet another painter and saying 'like pulling teeth'. If people were born with the ability to put things into words, they wouldn't become musicians either.

I'd never have read the biography of Les Murray if I hadn't remembered Bob Ellis saying, some time in the Nineties, 'but he's a *nice* Fascist'. If you're a real Aquarian, your first thought is nobody's wrong all the time. Les had taken to the forest years ago, back to *his* roots, and for a couple of months we exchanged deep thoughts on Neptune and crucified women. Today I'm sorry I didn't send him a postcard from Bcharre, Lebanon, the birthplace of Khalil Gibran. We'd never got around to discussing him, but being a Catholic Les would have loved the Qadisha Valley, all those Maronite hermits, and might have smiled too at the boys in the souped-up cars making the nights hideous, like Pauly and Habib in *Pizza*. Les had written his letters by hand, but surely he had television.

***

[56] Betty Sutton, ed, *Pioneer Families of Cooroy and District*, Cooroy-Noosa Genealogical and Historical Research Group Inc, 2002.

[57] Poul C Poulsen arrived in Sydney in 1876 and in 1882 moved to Queensland, opening his first studio in Queen Street, Brisbane, in 1885.

Chapter 19
Conclusion

'You should never ask an historian to predict the future – frankly, we have a hard enough time predicting the past.' --A J P Taylor

***

Of course it didn't all end there, as they're maybe thinking, me finally buying a .22 or worse and making possum stew from the Charleston Junior League recipe book, c.1950, before taking out the occupants of the five McMansions, or a goodly portion of Noosa. It's more that I realised burying a dead dingo is yet another thing that's a man's job (you'll find they increase with age) and that I'd become addicted to Fisher Library, the regular surge of adrenalin on finding yet another thing they'd prefer dead and buried.

That's another of their delusions, you can afford to come back, though it helped that the kid was now living with the real estate woman of the year. But I didn't expect to find myself headhunted a few months later by 2MBS-FM, in urgent need of an acting editor and recalling I'd once filled in over the Christmas break. I bought opera-going clothes and torturous heels, and within days found myself at a cocktail party chatting with David Malouf about Lebanon. He said his grandparents came from a place called Subtly in the Beqaa Valley

'Oh, what a shame', I said. 'I only got to Zarly. Pretty little place with old Ottoman houses and a main street called Rue Brasil because at one stage just about everybody emigrated.'

'That's it,' he smiled.

Obviously a case of lost in transliteration, as 'Zahle' written in Arabic has a hard T in the middle. But also of the universe having a quiet chuckle.

Kirsty the real estate genius was also responsible for my next Jewish boyfriend, though it depends how we're defining either word. As I've said, when it comes to exerting any influence a paternal grandmother ranks a distant second, and a paternal grandfather (the one responsible for the name I'd have killed for) tails the field.

Certainly he'd aspired to some degree of relationship on my sofa around midnight, after we'd watched *Wag the Dog* and sung one too many ancient university songs, after *Here's to Mrs Mac, Who keeps a house of amusement,* it was the one about owning brothels in Rio Janiero. But he was gently rebuffed, and when he rang next day saying he wasn't the man I was looking for, no doubt they imagine that as an educated woman I should be smart enough to tell him he wasn't the man any woman was looking for.

But deadline was approaching, still one strapline short and another reader's letter to invent replying to the person who'd thought it inappropriate that my predecessor had written so much about Teddy Tahu Rhodes' tatts and piercings.

Besides, I hadn't wanted to hurt his feelings. Rhodes Scholar, witty and amusing, understood opera (or rather, enough history to share my hatred of *Jenufa* on a collective farm, and transgendered Julius Caesar), and the only man I'd ever met capable of writing a rational op-ed on Israel. We just had irreconcilable differences about compulsory student unionism. Admittedly as an aged person I'd been exempt, but my argument was objective, whereas his was entirely subjective and emotional, based on memories of his glory days when university was like joining a club, jolly boating weather and close-run things on playing fields.

'It's not *like* that any more,' I said.

When what I ought to have said was that back then, there'd still been a *there* there.

***

There was a morning in Iran when the other two tour groups, the Belgians and the Austrians, must have preceded us on the road to Yadz and the Zoroastrian Towers of Silence, because our driver came back smiling from the_military checkpoint. 'Where are you taking all these old people?' they'd asked him, a reasonable question in a country where most people are under twenty-five. And although we'd laughed too, ('what old people? Matt, you're going to feed us to the vultures!') it didn't occur to us we could ask the Iranians where they're taking all their young people, the ones living in those ever-expanding beige concrete tenements south of Tehran.

What if it's an election year, or what passes for an election, and they take to the streets because you haven't delivered whatever you promised? Never dreaming it'll soon be a worldwide phenomenon.

Even by 2008, watching Philippe Petit walk audaciously between those shining towers in 1974, there's still something they're not getting, regarding *theres* which are no longer there. If the film can be believed, (and live on stage at the Cremorne Orpheum, he gave no indication that it couldn't) within the hour he's enjoying those carnal pleasures the terrorists could only anticipate, those seventy-two virgins they find so hilarious, forgetting we've been there done that ourselves, with Valkyries.

Back in the day when people glimpsed the previous gateway to paradise, the Statue of Liberty, gratification also came comparatively quickly. Look at Gatsby, only five years before he's gazing from his debt-free mansion at the green light at the end of Daisy's dock, whereas now it takes about twenty-five, most of them sitting still, before you can even get started. A quarter of a century that could well have been less about satisfying a love of learning (Aureliano, in *A Hundred Years of Solitude,* poring over the disintegrating parchments of Melquiades) than the ticking of little boxes, to ensure material success.

Yet how utterly rational it must have seemed at the time, that others would welcome salvation too, from what they themselves had come to despise. That everyone would want the same flavour of paradise as their own. Sally's 'I'll have what she's having!' when it was more like Henry Ford's 'Any colour as long it's black.'

So who knows what I'd believe if I hadn't escaped the great white whale, or whatever they're telling kids *Moby Dick* is a metaphor for? (My grandsons haven't asked me to comment on their assignments after the one where they said Dracula was about gender oppression.)

But one metaphor everyone gets is being burnt by the sun, and how irrational is it to think that when its light, around 1979, reached Neptune only through a dark Plutonian prism, the people who aspired to change the world forgot what Ollie was trying to show me, the patient woman in the sea green dress, and could imagine no other way than force and compulsion?

I'm not saying the Beatles were right, *all you need is love,* or that Oscar Wilde was either, despite being Irish, that each man kills the thing he loves. But with the Middle East, a bit of love, *ahavta, alhab,* along with propinquity, would have gone a long way. And just as Islamic Studies, post 9/11, became the new box to tick for people who knew nothing of rose-red cities and Ozymandias, the *Mu'allaqat* and the magically echoing mosques, and cared less, so it was after WW2, which arguably was a continuation of WW1 when the horse was defeated by technology.

True, from a military perspective donkeys and carrier

pigeons no longer had a future either, but it's the disappearance of the horse, not just from battlefields but from our emotional landscape, that was the great ecological mistake, worse than introducing the cane toad or removing wolves from Yellowstone – or dictators from Syria and Libya. Today they'll tell you Lawrence of Arabia was the hopeless romantic, falling in love with galloping Bedouins, but there wouldn't have been nearly as much *verschlimmbessering* if they, the rational ones, hadn't become entranced by Kemal Ataturk.

Admittedly there's no images of Ataturk astride a horse at Gallipoli, but there's equestrian statues of him clear across Turkey and The Man on Horseback is yet another metaphor, what they call a trope, and Samuel Finer's eponymous book, subtitled *The Role of the Military in Politics,* with an introductory quote from *Don Giovanni,* was one of several in Fisher Library which made it pretty clear that by the 1920s it wasn't just my mother, yearning for a man who danced divinely (which Ataturk did, and possibly played a decent game of tennis too, though he treated his women dreadfully – even Bill Clinton never had a mistress who shot herself in the Rose Garden).

She was simply in tune with the *zeitgeist*, men and women who hungered for heroes but who lacked the capacity for discernment, and possibly for love. Who never bothered learning Arabic, Farsi or Turkish, or ventured too far from hotels serving whatever all salads were served with before Thousand Island dressing. Imagining one part of the Middle East was much the same as another, nothing that couldn't be fixed by technology and a decent military dictator (though technically Ataturk wasn't), and shaped in their own image.

***

Like my parents a century earlier, I haven't the foggiest what I was doing on 28 June 2014, the centenary of Sarajevo, but the previous Christmas, or it could have been the one before, Ollie came up for the big family lunch, at the house of his widowed brother in Northbridge, appearing in the kitchen just as I was setting out my Lebanese fennel wafers and pickled lemon guacamole.

'You're looking more like Cardinal Pell than ever,' I said, as the bilingual Norwegian tots, still jetlagged, scampered under our feet. I knew what'd happen if I mentioned my two *bisnietos* up in Cairns, whose grandfather, the one who wasn't a Basque terrorist after all, might already be reading them my Christmas present, *The Gruffalo's Child*.

'*Él es muy, muy grande? Es muy muy malo?*'

But either Ollie hadn't heard me, or the weather had put him in a mellow mood – overcast and dampish, what we Irish call a soft day – as I escaped a lecture on enunciating my consonants. And it wasn't long before he started nipping out to the terrace for a smoke, careful not to ash in the terracotta strawberry pots, so to show solidarity (That Woman!) and stay clear of Deirdre who now had even more reason to detest me, eighty-four and not even a grandmother, I'd go out and encourage him to remember filthy limericks about the bishop of Birmingham, along with old and useless things, like when we first saw *War and Peace* and why Jersey cows were more ferocious. What creosote was used for, and the smell of the green ointment we used for girthgall.

Boxing Day was lunch with the kids, which happens once in a blue moon, at a Spanish restaurant where not everyone gets to hear Ollie's limericks, whispered discreetly over the suckling pig. The grandsons show promise, but the threshold gets ever higher – eighteen and still not allowed a sip of sauvignon blanc! But Bruno Bettelheim was right about crazy third sons coming good, now the kid's started film school it's *noir* from morning to night, he can't get enough of Greek myths and heroic quests.

And pretty soon it's Jeremy Clarkson and football and with both daughters-in-law, the white and the brown, too far away, Buckley's chance of imparting useful advice about Cavafy's Laestrygonians, that as big and bad as they are, and as small as they'll try to make you feel, you must remember this, the loser is the one who forgets when they *need* to be afraid. Whether it's boiling frogs or the people in the Goya painting, or the Archduke Ferdinand in Sarajevo, unaware his wedding anniversary coincides with the First Battle of Kosovo and triggering a four year war or a thirty-one year war, depending on your perspective. A watershed moment anyway, like the one I'd hoped to tell the grandchildren about Morocco.

I'd arrived in Casablanca a day early, as had my roommate Jade who'd already met a gorgeous Aussie guy who was about to manage a bar for some American woman. So *faute de mieux* I set out with Jade down Rue Muhammad V, watching my step on the usual dodgy kerbing and guttering and making a note of flaking Art Deco cinemas to explore later, to meet him for coffee and agree it beats going back to being a tax inspector in Sydney. When suddenly, there in the White Lotus Café, it's a lightbulb moment, realising it's not any old bar, but a faithful replica of Rick's Café being gloriously born, somewhat behind schedule due to Ramadan, on Sour Djid Street. The one which was only ever a film set in Hollywood.

'Oh, like you guys mean like there was a *film* called *Casablanca?*' says Jade.

So there is something to write about after all, the world being reshaped in the nicest possible way, and as Kathy Kriger tells me next day, you would, wouldn't you? If for the last sixty years millions of tourists have been sneered at for asking where it is, obviously it *ought* to be there, so make it happen! How else can she keep on living in a place she loves when she hasn't enough super to retire on?

So remember this too. Don't laugh at people who see things that aren't there, or which once existed, or happened, only they've forgotten them, as happens ever faster in a shrinking world. They'll happen again, same only different. So pay attention, show a little more respect, at best love, for the past.

It won't necessarily help you to predict the future, but you'll be less surprised by the present.

***